SELF-IMAGE MENTAL HEALTH EMOTIONS

PSYCHOLOGY
for Curious Kids

An illustrated introduction to brain science, identity, mental health—and more!

DECISION-MAKING

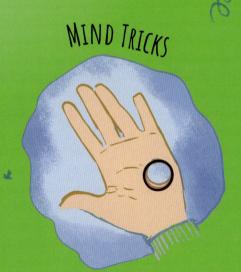
MIND TRICKS

ARCTURUS

ARCTURUS

This edition published in 2025 by Arcturus Publishing Limited
26/27 Bickels Yard, 151–153 Bermondsey Street,
London SE1 3HA

Copyright © Arcturus Holdings Limited

All rights reserved. No part of this publication may be reproduced, stored in a retrieval system, or transmitted, in any form or by any means, electronic, mechanical, photocopying, recording, or otherwise, without prior written permission in accordance with the provisions of the Copyright Act 1956 (as amended). Any person or persons who do any unauthorized act in relation to this publication may be liable to criminal prosecution and civil claims for damages.

Author: Anna Claybourne
Illustrator: Nik Neves
Designer: Dani Leigh
Managing designer: Rosie Bellwood-Moyler
Consultant: Emily Ralls
Editor: Lydia Halliday
Managing editor: Joe Harris

ISBN: 978-1-3988-5050-7
CH011588US
Supplier 29, Date 0225, PI 00009007
Printed in China

What is STEM?
STEM is a world-wide initiative that aims to cultivate an interest in Science, Technology, Engineering, and Mathematics, in an effort to promote these disciplines to as wide a variety of students as possible.

CONTENTS

THE BRAIN AND THE MIND.............5

THINKING LIKE A HUMAN 6

CHAPTER 1:

HOW THE BRAIN WORKS 9

MEET YOUR BRAIN 10

BRAIN CELLS..................................12

BRAIN AND BODY 14

WHAT'S GOING ON? 16

STORING MEMORIES......................18

SLEEP AND DREAMING...................20

STUDYING THE BRAIN....................22

BRAIN MYTHS AND MYSTERIES.......24

CHAPTER 2:

WHAT IS THE MIND? 27

LAYERS OF THE MIND 28

MEMORIES AND THE MIND.............30

THINKING THOUGHTS 32

PERCEPTION 34

EMOTIONS....................................36

PERSONALITY 38

INTELLIGENCE 40

NEURODIVERSITY 42

CHAPTER 3:

HUMAN BEHAVIOR 45

ANCIENT IDEAS............................46

WHO AM I?...................................48

SPEECH AND LANGUAGE 50

NONVERBAL COMMUNICATION...52

GROUPS 54

INFLUENCING EACH OTHER 56

MAKING MISTAKES 58

ANIMALS AND US 60

CHAPTER 4:

GROWING AND CHANGING 63

HOW THE BRAIN EVOLVED.............64

NATURE AND NURTURE..................66

BABY BRAINS 68

CHILDHOOD CHANGES.................70

TEENAGE BRAINS..........................72

THE ADULT BRAIN 74

GETTING OLDER 76

OLDER AGE 78

CHAPTER 5:

BRAIN EXPERIMENTS 81

HOW IT STARTED..........................82

HOW EXPERIMENTS WORK............84

ANIMAL EXPERIMENTS 86

BABIES AND CHILDREN.................88

PERCEPTION EXPERIMENTS 90

THE INFLUENCE OF OTHERS...........92

MEMORY TESTS.............................94

COMPUTER MODELS 96

AMAZING EFFECTS........................98

CHAPTER 6:

MENTAL HEALTH AND ILLNESS 101

FEELING STRESSED!........................102

TYPES OF MENTAL ILLNESSES.........104

WHAT CAUSES MENTAL ILLNESS?.106

TREATMENTS AND THERAPIES........108

MIND MEDICINE 110

BRAIN DAMAGE 112

BRAIN SURGERY 114

STAYING HEALTHY 116

PERFORMANCE PSYCHOLOGY.......118

INTO THE FUTURE.........................120

BRAIN EXPERIMENTS 122

GLOSSARY....................................124

INDEX 126

 # THE BRAIN AND THE MIND

What's inside your head? First, your head is mainly filled with your brain, an amazingly clever and complicated organ that controls the rest of your body. But "what's inside your head" can also mean your mind. Your mind means who you are—your personality, memories, likes and dislikes, thoughts, ideas, and feelings.

Psychology is the science of the brain and the mind. Psychologists study how the brain works and how it does things like store memories, experience what's going on around you, make decisions, or conjure things up in your "mind's eye."

When we think, feel, or imagine things, signals are zooming around between the billions of cells that make up the brain. But how does that make us able to experience, understand, and think about things in the way we do? How do our brains and minds help us to talk, get along with others, solve problems, or dream up stories or inventions? How can signals in your brain make you experience the color orange, dance to your favorite song, or recognize a face? And how do our brains and minds change as we grow up?

You'll find many of the answers in this book—but not all! That's because there are still some questions about the brain and mind that remain mysterious and are waiting for scientists to solve them …

THINKING LIKE A HUMAN

We humans are animals—just like dogs and cats, elephants, fish, and butterflies. Like them, we move around, look for food, and reproduce (have babies). But there's a big difference between us and other animals—a big BRAIN difference!

THE HUMAN BRAIN

Human brains are thought to be the most powerful of any animal species. Though human brains aren't the biggest of all, they have the most cells in the thinking part of the brain and the most connections between them.

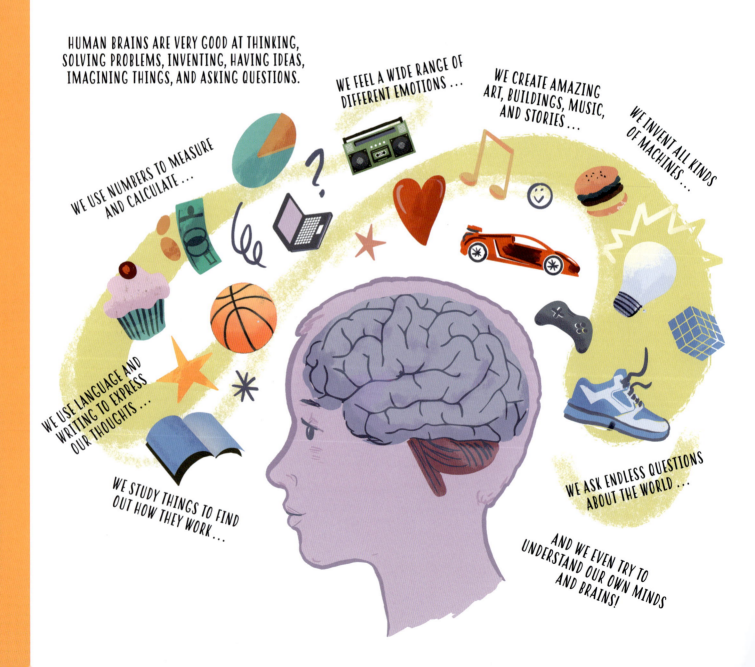

HUMAN BRAINS ARE VERY GOOD AT THINKING, SOLVING PROBLEMS, INVENTING, HAVING IDEAS, IMAGINING THINGS, AND ASKING QUESTIONS.

WE FEEL A WIDE RANGE OF DIFFERENT EMOTIONS...

WE CREATE AMAZING ART, BUILDINGS, MUSIC, AND STORIES...

WE INVENT ALL KINDS OF MACHINES...

WE USE NUMBERS TO MEASURE AND CALCULATE...

WE USE LANGUAGE AND WRITING TO EXPRESS OUR THOUGHTS...

WE STUDY THINGS TO FIND OUT HOW THEY WORK...

WE ASK ENDLESS QUESTIONS ABOUT THE WORLD...

AND WE EVEN TRY TO UNDERSTAND OUR OWN MINDS AND BRAINS!

UNDERSTANDING OURSELVES

We've been trying to make sense of our own thoughts, behavior, feelings, and actions since ancient times. Poets and philosophers have always talked about them ...

ANCIENT GREEK POET SAPPHO

"WHAT SHOULD I DO? I AM IN TWO MINDS!"

"HE WHO LEARNS BUT DOES NOT THINK, IS LOST!"

ANCIENT CHINESE PHILOSOPHER KONG QUI, OR CONFUCIUS

"OH, FULL OF SCORPIONS IS MY MIND!"

ENGLISH PLAYWRIGHT WILLIAM SHAKESPEARE EXPLORED THE MIND IN PLAYS SUCH AS *MACBETH*.

More recently, we've started to study the brain and mind using science. Psychology is the study of the mind, how we behave, our feelings, and personalities. Another science—neuroscience—studies how the brain works and its links to the body.

WHO *DOES* HAVE THE BIGGEST BRAIN OF ALL?

That's the sperm whale, with a brain roughly the size of a beach ball! Sperm whales are smart, but their brains are still smaller compared to the rest of their bodies than human brains are.

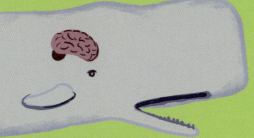

HUMAN BRAIN: ABOUT 1.5 KG (3.3 LB)—ABOUT ONE-40TH OF A HUMAN'S WEIGHT.

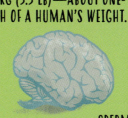

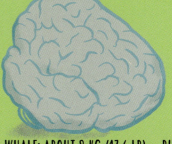

SPERM WHALE: ABOUT 8 KG (17.6 LB)—BUT THAT'S ONLY ONE-5,000TH OF THE WHALE'S WEIGHT.

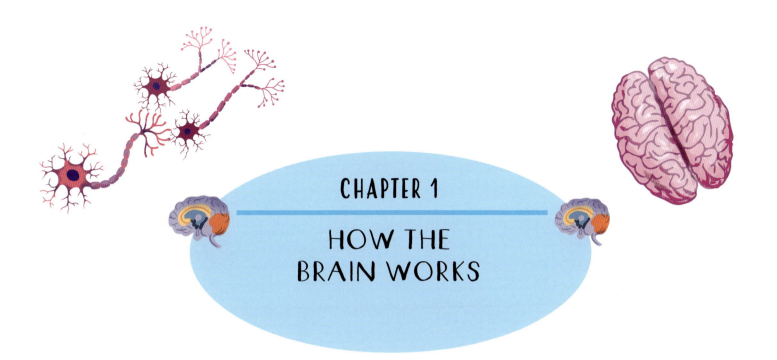

CHAPTER 1

HOW THE BRAIN WORKS

If you could look at your brain right now, you'd see a jellylike, pinkish-gray lump about the size of a large coconut. The surface of the brain isn't smooth, but covered in deep folds and wrinkles. And underneath, toward the back, is the brain stem, a kind of stalk that connects the brain to the rest of the body.

Somewhere inside this strange-looking lump are all your thoughts, feelings, ideas, memories, and experiences—as well as all the brain parts that control your breathing, sleep, and heartbeat, make your muscles move, and tell you when you're hungry, thirsty, tired, or need to visit the bathroom! But how? In this chapter, we'll explore what's in the brain and how it works.

MEET YOUR BRAIN

Though the brain looks as if it's made of wobbly jelly, it's not the same all the way through. It has different layers and parts inside that do different jobs.

ON THE OUTSIDE

Most of the brain is covered in a surface layer called the cortex. It's much more than just a skin—it's actually one of the most important parts of the brain. It's the part you use for thinking, understanding, sensing the world, and making decisions.

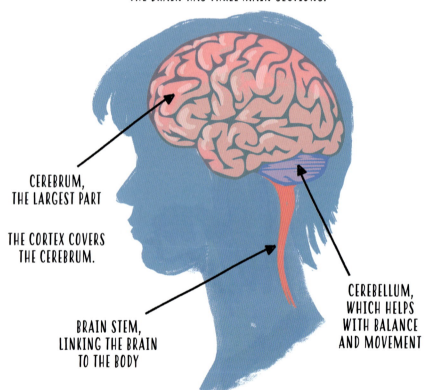

THE BRAIN HAS THREE MAIN SECTIONS:

CEREBRUM, THE LARGEST PART

THE CORTEX COVERS THE CEREBRUM.

BRAIN STEM, LINKING THE BRAIN TO THE BODY

CEREBELLUM, WHICH HELPS WITH BALANCE AND MOVEMENT

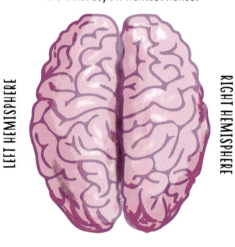

THE CEREBRUM AND CORTEX HAVE TWO HALVES, OR HEMISPHERES.

LEFT HEMISPHERE

RIGHT HEMISPHERE

OUT OF CURIOSITY
The cortex is wrinkled and folded up, so that it can fit inside your head. If it was spread out flat, it would be about the size of a newspaper.

Chapter 1

10

CORTEX AREAS

Different areas of the cortex deal with different things. This picture shows the main areas and what they do.

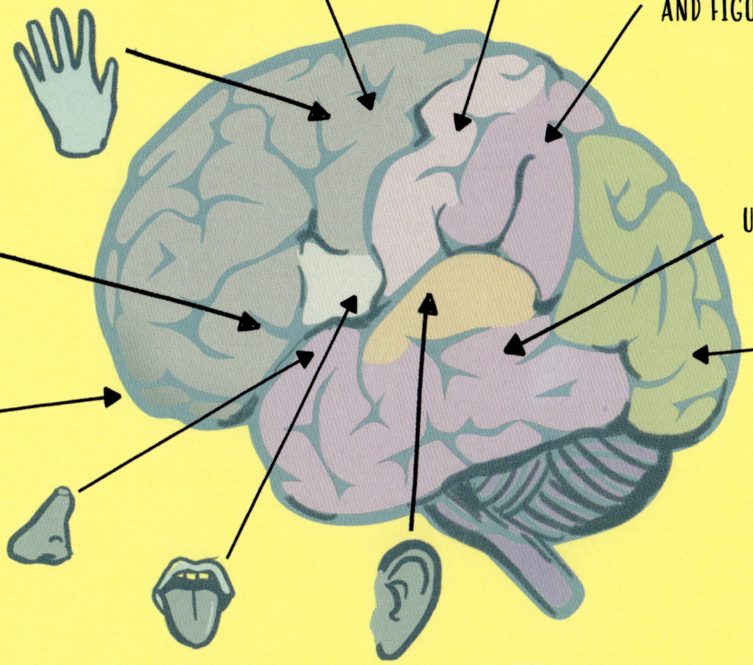

SENSORY CORTEX
RECEIVING TOUCH SIGNALS FROM DIFFERENT PARTS OF THE BODY

MOTOR CORTEX
SENDING SIGNALS TO THE MUSCLES

SENSORY ASSOCIATION AREA
MAKING SENSE OF TOUCH SENSATIONS AND FIGURING OUT YOUR POSITION

BROCA'S AREA
PLANNING AND USING LANGUAGE

WERNICKE'S AREA
UNDERSTANDING LANGUAGE

PREFRONTAL CORTEX
THINKING, PLANNING, PROBLEM-SOLVING, AND MAKING DECISIONS

VISUAL CORTEX
MAKING SENSE OF SIGNALS FROM YOUR EYES AND FIGURING OUT WHAT YOU'RE LOOKING AT

OLFACTORY (SMELL) AREA
PROCESSING SMELL SIGNALS

TASTE AREA
PROCESSING TASTE SIGNALS

AUDITORY (HEARING) AREA
PROCESSING SOUND SIGNALS FROM THE EARS

ON THE INSIDE

Deep inside the brain is the limbic system. It also has two sides, and each side has several important parts.

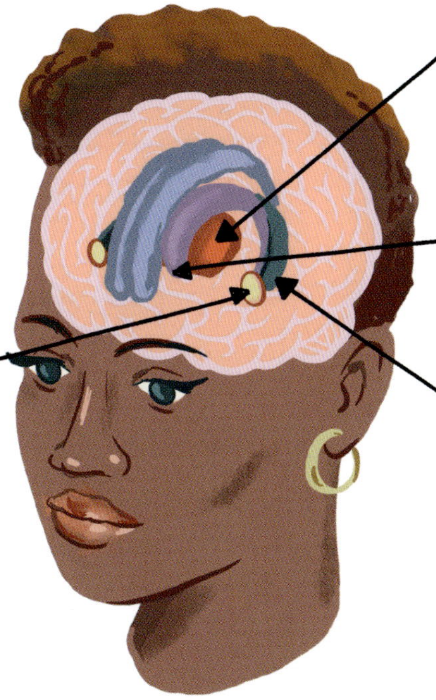

THALAMUS
SORTS OUT INFORMATION COMING INTO THE BRAIN AND SENDS IT TO DIFFERENT AREAS OF THE CORTEX

HYPOTHALAMUS
HELPS TO CONTROL SLEEP, HUNGER, THIRST, BODY TEMPERATURE, AND EMOTIONS

AMYGDALA
CONTROLS STRONG, BASIC EMOTIONS INCLUDING FEAR AND ANGER

HIPPOCAMPUS
SORTS OUT MEMORIES AND HELPS TO DECIDE WHAT TO FORGET AND WHAT TO STORE

 # BRAIN CELLS

Like other body parts, the brain is made up of cells. There are two main types: neurons, which carry signals, and glial cells, which support the neurons.

NEURONS

Neurons are the brain cells that carry signals around inside the brain and between the brain and the body. They are the cells we use to think, understand, remember, and imagine things.

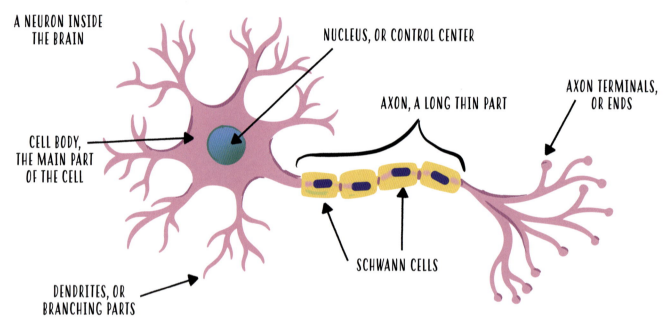

A NEURON INSIDE THE BRAIN

NUCLEUS, OR CONTROL CENTER

AXON, A LONG THIN PART

AXON TERMINALS, OR ENDS

CELL BODY, THE MAIN PART OF THE CELL

SCHWANN CELLS

DENDRITES, OR BRANCHING PARTS

GLIAL CELLS

There are many more glial cells than neurons. They do jobs like controlling blood flow and other liquids in the brain, or holding neurons in place. Some, called Schwann cells, surround the axons of neurons to help them transmit signals.

BRAIN CELL FACTS
Number of neurons in the cortex: About 16 billion
Total number of neurons in the brain: Over 80 billion
Total number of brain cells: About 170 billion
Number of connections: 100 TRILLION (that's 1,000,000,000,000)

LINKING TOGETHER

In your brain, signals travel around by zooming along neurons, then jumping from one neuron to another. The link between two neurons is called a synapse.

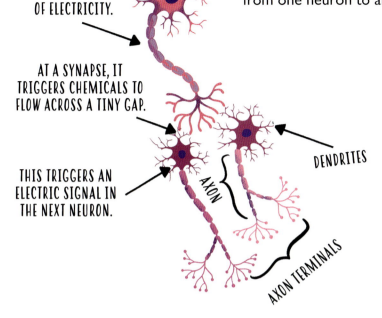

A SIGNAL TRAVELS ALONG A NEURON AS A TINY AMOUNT OF ELECTRICITY.

AT A SYNAPSE, IT TRIGGERS CHEMICALS TO FLOW ACROSS A TINY GAP.

THIS TRIGGERS AN ELECTRIC SIGNAL IN THE NEXT NEURON.

DENDRITES
AXON
AXON TERMINALS

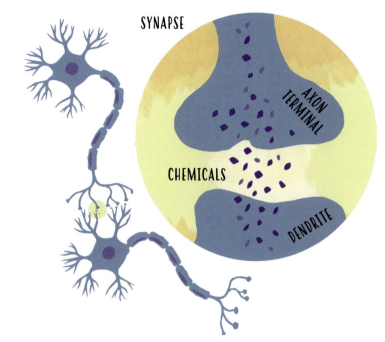

SYNAPSE
AXON TERMINAL
CHEMICALS
DENDRITE

BRAIN CELL NETWORK

Each neuron is microscopic and too small to see. And there are billions and billions of them in your brain. One neuron can have thousands of dendrites and be linked to thousands of other neurons. Together, they form an incredibly complicated network.

Try thinking about something, such as an elephant riding a motorcycle, what you had for breakfast, or the answer to 3 x 7. As you do this, signals are zipping around inside your brain, jumping from one neuron to the next along many different pathways.

GRAY AND WHITE MATTER

The ends of the neurons mainly cluster together near the surface of the brain, while the axons can reach from one area to another. This gives the brain two layers, known as gray matter and white matter.

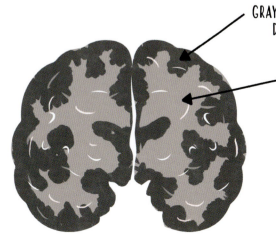

GRAY MATTER MADE OF CELL BODIES, DENDRITES, AND TERMINALS

WHITE MATTER MADE OF BUNDLES OF AXONS

Chapter 1

13

BRAIN AND BODY

Your brain is connected to your body, so that messages and signals can travel between them. The two are connected together by a big network of pathways called nerves.

THE NERVOUS SYSTEM

In this diagram, you can see how nerves join the brain to every part of the body. Together, the brain and nerves are called the nervous system.

The brain stem links the brain to the spinal cord. This is a big bundle of nerves that runs down your back, inside your backbone. These parts make up the central nervous system.

More nerves branch off from the spinal cord and connect to your arms and legs, bones and muscles, the organs inside you, and to the skin all over your body. These nerves are called the peripheral nervous system.

CENTRAL NERVOUS SYSTEM
BRAIN
SPINAL CORD
PERIPHERAL NERVOUS SYSTEM
NERVES

OUT OF CURIOSITY

Remember how the brain has two halves, or hemispheres?

Strangely, the right brain hemisphere mostly controls the left side of the body, while the left hemisphere controls the right side.

NERVE CELLS

Nerves are made up of bundles of neurons, the same type of cells that carry signals inside the brain. Sensory neurons link the sense organs, such as touch sensors in the skin, to the spinal cord and brain. Another type of neuron, motor neurons, link the brain to muscles and other structures in your body.

A TOUCH-SENSING SENSORY NEURON

A MOTOR NEURON CONNECTING TO A MUSCLE

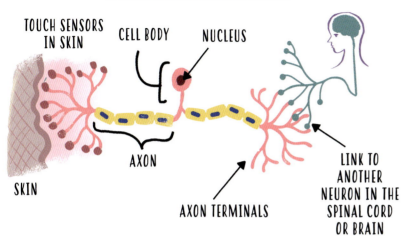

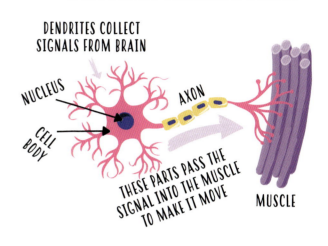

SIGNALS IN, SIGNALS OUT!

Sensory neurons pass information to your brain from your senses, so it knows what's happening around you. Motor neurons carry signals to your muscles so that you can react.

For example, imagine that you touch a sharp cactus.

1. PAIN SENSORS IN YOUR FINGERTIP SEND SIGNALS ALONG SENSORY NEURONS.
2. THE SIGNALS TRAVEL UP THE SPINAL CORD INTO THE BRAIN.
3. NEURONS INSIDE THE BRAIN FIGURE OUT WHAT'S HAPPENING.
4. THE BRAIN NEURONS SEND A SIGNAL ALONG A MOTOR NEURON TO YOUR MUSCLES...
5. ...MAKING YOU PULL YOUR HAND AWAY!

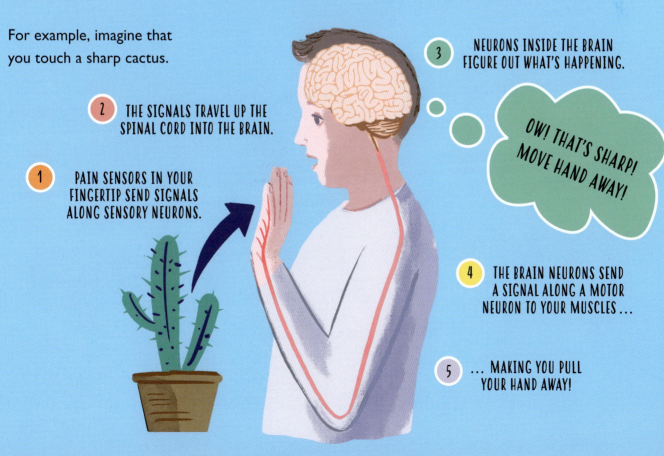

Chapter 1

15

WHAT'S GOING ON?

Your senses of sight, hearing, touch, taste, and smell tell your brain what's happening around you. But the information they send isn't enough on its own. The brain has to process it, or sort it out and make sense of it, by comparing it to what it already knows.

WHAT WORDS MEAN

One example is what happens when someone is talking to you. Words and other sounds have no meaning on their own. Your brain has to process them and make sense of what they mean to you.

1. WHEN SOMEONE SPEAKS, IT MAKES SOUND WAVES THAT MAKE THE AIR VIBRATE.

2. YOUR EARS DETECT THE PATTERN OF VIBRATIONS...

3. ...AND SEND SIGNALS ALONG NERVES TO YOUR BRAIN.

4. YOUR BRAIN COMPARES THE PATTERNS TO SOUND PATTERNS IT HAS HEARD BEFORE.

5. IT MATCHES THEM UP TO THE MEANINGS YOU HAVE STORED FOR THEM IN YOUR MEMORY.

6. AND THEN IT FIGURES OUT HOW YOU FEEL ABOUT THAT!

❓ UPSIDE-DOWN EYES

Signals from your eyes need even more processing. The way your eyes work means that your image of the world gets flipped upside down and back to front inside your eyeballs.

But you don't see everything upside down, do you? That's because your brain rearranges the information from your eyes and "flips" it back again.

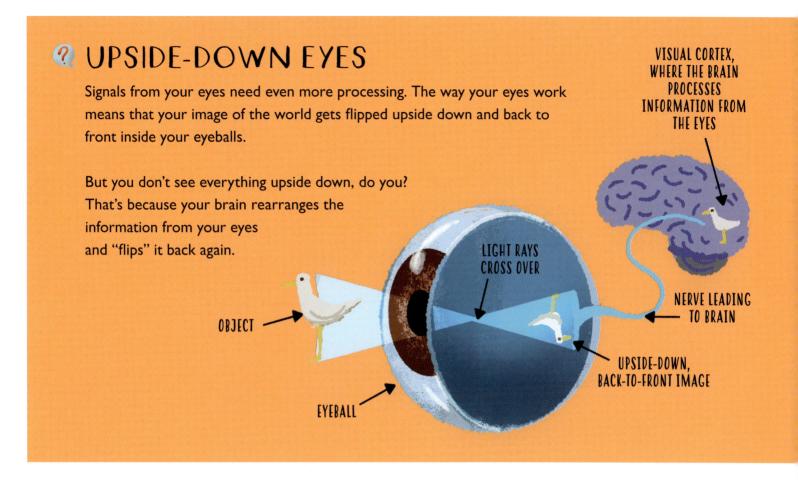

❓ FILTERING

Your brain can also "filter out" information you don't need. For example, if a room has a funny smell, you'll notice when you first go in. But after a while, your brain starts to ignore it, and you stop noticing it. That leaves your brain free to look for new, useful information. You can also filter out sounds—such as when you're in a busy cafe with music playing.

All the sounds you can hear are mixed together into a pattern of sound waves entering your ears. But your brain can pick out one person's voice and tune out the rest!

STORING MEMORIES

Your brain is stuffed full of memories.
Even if you don't think you have a good memory—you do!

WHAT'S IN THERE?

Memories aren't just events you remember, like a summer vacation. Your memory includes all the things you've learned and stored away since you were born, such as …

ALL THE SHAPES, LETTERS, NUMBERS, AND WORDS YOU KNOW

HOW TO WALK, TALK, SWIM, RIDE A BIKE, OR DANCE

STORIES, SONGS, GAMES, IDEAS, DREAMS, AND PLANS

AND THINGS THAT ARE IMPORTANT MEMORIES FOR YOU, LIKE A GREAT BIRTHDAY PARTY, OR SOMETHING THAT SCARED YOU

HOW TO DO EVERYDAY THINGS LIKE TIE SHOELACES, COOK PASTA, OR MAKE A PAPER PLANE

ALL THE OBJECTS, FACES, SOUNDS, TASTES, SMELLS AND OTHER THINGS YOU CAN RECOGNIZE

SCRAP OR SAVE?

Why do we forget lots of things, but remember other things forever? It's because we have different types of memory.

Short-term memory holds a small amount of stuff for a short time—things like someone telling you their phone number. You remember it for a few seconds, but soon forget it.

Working memory is used to store the information you're using or working on. If you're playing a game, your working memory keeps track of everyone's moves and your strategy.

Long-term memory stores long-lasting memories. Things that are important to you or that are repeated a lot, move into your long-term memory—such as learning your favorite song, for example.

WHERE ARE YOUR MEMORIES?

To store a memory, the network of neurons in your brain changes, making new connections, or making connections stronger, and forming new neuron patterns and pathways. When you remember something, signals zoom along the same pathways again. Your brain has several places to store memories.

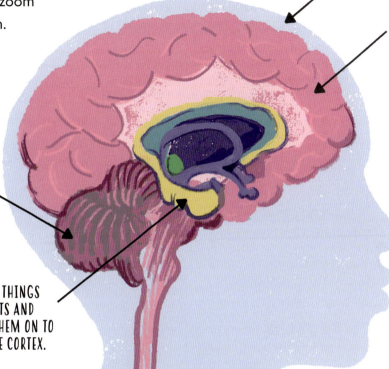

LONG-TERM MEMORIES CAN BE STORED ALL OVER THE CORTEX.

THE PREFRONTAL CORTEX HOLDS SHORT-TERM AND WORKING MEMORY.

THE CEREBELLUM HELPS WITH MOVEMENTS, AND STORES "MUSCLE MEMORY"—AUTOMATIC SEQUENCES OF MOVEMENTS YOU USE FOR THINGS LIKE PLAYING AN INSTRUMENT OR WRITING.

THE HIPPOCAMPUS STORES THINGS THAT HAPPEN TO YOU, FACTS AND INFORMATION, AND PASSES THEM ON TO LONG-TERM MEMORY IN THE CORTEX.

MEMORY TRICKS

It's easier for things to stick in your memory if you link them together into a story, pattern, or visual image.

Imagine that you needed to remember this shopping list ...

—Dog food

—Ice cream

—Bananas

—Sunscreen

Connect all the items together into a funny picture, and it's easier to memorize them.

Chapter 1

19

SLEEP AND DREAMING

The average person spends 24 years of their life sleeping. But why do we do it? Neuroscientists think that sleep allows the brain and body time to rest, recharge, and reorder—so that we start the new day feeling healthy and happy.

FALLING ASLEEP

Although it's not always easy to fall asleep, our brain works hard to help us do this. The suprachiasmatic nucleus (SCN) is a cluster of neurons in the hypothalamus (see page 11). It is the brain's clock. It keeps track of time, so that key activities—such as feeling sleepy and hungry—happen at about the same times each day. The SCN also gets signals from your eyes, along the optic nerve. As your eyes signal that darkness is falling, the SCN signals to the pineal gland. This gland produces the hormone melatonin, which makes you feel sleepy.

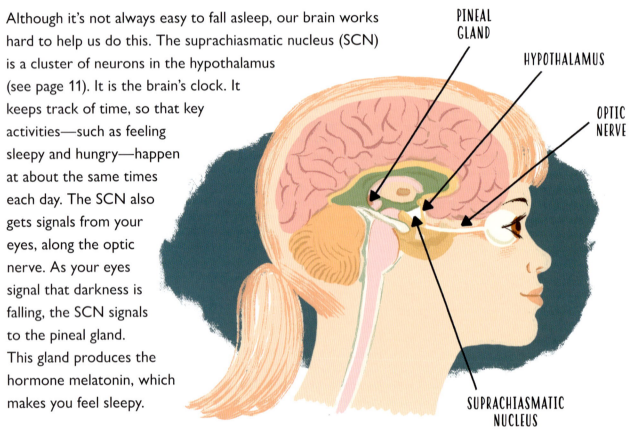

DREAMING

Whether or not you remember your dreams, you dream three to five times per night. You dream only during a type of sleep called REM (short for "rapid eye movement," because it makes your eyes move quickly under your closed eyelids). During REM, your brain sorts out what you have seen and felt during the day. As it stores information needed for the future, you experience a mishmash of images and ideas.

SLEEP STAGES

Neuroscientists divide sleep into REM sleep and three stages of non-REM sleep. Non-REM sleep is dreamless and allows your brain to rest. Not getting enough of either REM or non-REM sleep can make you tired, irritable, and less able to think clearly. As you drift off to sleep, entering Stage 1 of non-REM, your brain shuts down some activities, so you are no longer aware of your surroundings. Your muscles relax, and your breathing slows. Each non-REM stage is deeper than the last: Stage 2 is deeper than Stage 1, and Stage 3 is deepest of all. You usually have three to five sleep cycles every night, moving through non-REM and REM each time.

OUT OF CURIOSITY

To feel well rested, most adults need around 8 hours of sleep a night, but children need between 9 and 12 hours.

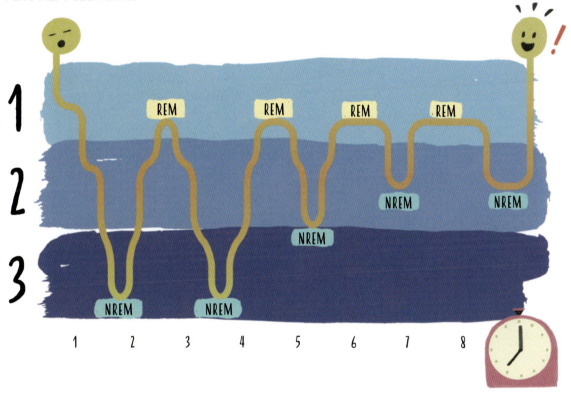

WAKING UP

Even if you are not woken by an alarm clock, you may find yourself waking at around the same time each morning. This is because your SCN has kept track of time throughout the night. In the morning, it may also get signals that sunlight is shining through your closed eyelids. The SCN tells the pineal gland to stop making melatonin, so you then start to wake up!

STUDYING THE BRAIN

Neuroscientists have several kinds of high-tech equipment to help them look closely at neurons and other brain parts.

THROUGH THE MICROSCOPE

Scientists can use a powerful microscope, such as an SEM (Scanning Electron Microscope) or a confocal microscope, to look at neurons and see the links and networks they form.

THE NEURONS IN THE SAMPLE REFLECT THE ELECTRONS IN DIFFERENT DIRECTIONS.

AN SEM FIRES A BEAM OF TINY PARTICLES CALLED ELECTRONS AT A SAMPLE OF BRAIN TISSUE.

A DETECTOR COLLECTS THE REFLECTED ELECTRONS AND TURNS THEM INTO A COMPUTER IMAGE.

COLORS ARE ADDED TO MAKE THE PARTS EASIER TO SEE.

OUT OF CURIOSITY
As well as helping to show how the brain works, brain wave patterns can reveal some brain illnesses, such as epilepsy (see page 114), and can help scientists study neurodivergent conditions such as ADHD (see page 43).

🔍 BRAIN SCANS

Scientists can also see people's brains working using fMRI (functional Magnetic Resonance Imaging). An fMRI machine surrounds your brain with very powerful (but harmless) magnetism and radio waves. They can detect which parts of your brain are using the most oxygen, showing where the neurons are most active, when you are doing different things.

AN FMRI SCANNER

THIS FMRI SCAN SHOWS WHICH PARTS OF THE BRAIN WERE MOST ACTIVE WHEN SOMEONE WAS READING WORDS.

WERNICKE'S AREA, USED FOR UNDERSTANDING LANGUAGE

VISUAL CORTEX, USED FOR PROCESSING SIGNALS FROM YOUR EYES

PARTS OF THE PREFRONTAL CORTEX, USED FOR THINKING ABOUT THINGS

🔍 BRAIN WAVES

People sometimes say "I've had a brain wave!" meaning a brilliant idea. But brain waves aren't actually ideas—they're electrical signals in your brain. Neurons work using small amounts of electricity. The strength of the electricity goes up and down at different speeds, depending on what you're doing.

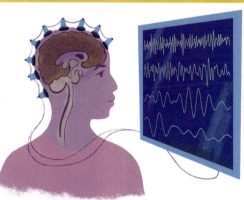

TO MEASURE BRAIN WAVES, SENSORS CALLED ELECTRODES ARE PUT AROUND THE HEAD. THEY PICK UP THE PATTERNS OF ELECTRICAL ENERGY AND SHOW THEM AS WAVES ON A SCREEN.

TYPES OF BRAIN WAVES

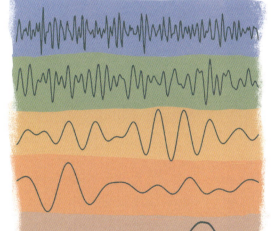

GAMMA—THINKING FAST, OR CONCENTRATING HARD

BETA—BUSY THINKING, TALKING, OR WORKING

ALPH—RELAXED AND CALM

THETA—DEEP RELAXATION, MEDITATION, OR DAYDREAMING

DELTA—DEEP SLEEP OR BEING UNCONSCIOUS

BRAIN MYTHS AND MYSTERIES

Neuroscientists have discovered a lot about the brain. But there are still mysteries about how our brains work—and several myths and misunderstandings, too.

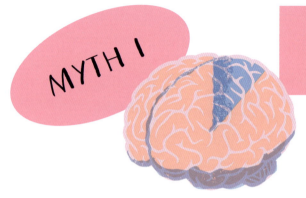

MYTH 1

YOU ONLY USE 10% OF YOUR BRAIN!

FALSE!

You use all your brain cells, and the whole brain is busy all the time—though some parts can be more active than others, depending on what you're doing.

MYTH 2

YOU CAN BE "LEFT-BRAINED" OR "RIGHT-BRAINED"

FALSE!

It is true that the two brain hemispheres are slightly different. For example, the left side deals more with language, and the right side is used more for pictures. But the two hemispheres are connected and work together, and we all use both of them.

MYTH 3

LISTENING TO CLASSICAL MUSIC—ESPECIALLY MOZART—MAKES YOU SMARTER

FALSE!

One scientist found that listening to music by the composer Mozart made people do slightly better at some tasks—but only for a few minutes! That doesn't mean it actually makes you smarter or better at learning.

BRAIN MYSTERIES

How do neurons encode information?
We know that neurons store information by forming connections—but we haven't figured out exactly how, or what each piece of information looks like in the brain.

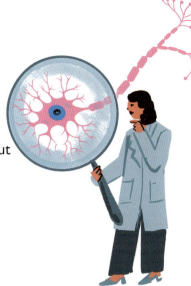

What is consciousness?
Being "conscious" means that we know we are thinking. We can think about ourselves, our thoughts and feelings, and be aware that we're doing that. But how can a bunch of brain cells make that happen? Nobody knows!

Phantom limbs

When people lose a limb, they can often still "feel" it—even though it's not there. That's probably because the brain still has the neurons that used to get sense signals from the missing limb. But it's not clear how this makes you feel that the phantom limb still exists.

Deja vu (French for "already seen")
This is the weird feeling that you've experienced something exactly the same way before—like a sentence someone says or a sequence of events. There are lots of theories about it, but we don't know why it happens.

ONE THING, OR TWO?
Some people think that the mind is part of the brain and can't exist without it. Others believe that the mind is a separate thing, sometimes called the "soul" or "spirit," that can exist without your body—an idea known as dualism.

Chapter 1

25

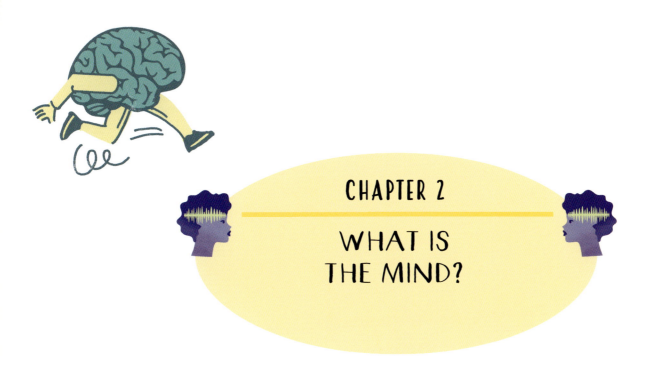

CHAPTER 2

WHAT IS THE MIND?

Your mind is the "you" that lives inside your head. It's made up of your personality, thoughts, feelings, memories, experiences, and awareness. It's always busy, thinking and feeling, experiencing what's going around you, learning new things, and changing over time. It's even there while you sleep, in the form of your dreams.

In this chapter, we'll look at how the mind works, how thinking, feeling, and experiencing things happen. There are different ideas about what the mind really is, and different people's minds can work in different ways—so this is a fascinating, mysterious, and sometimes puzzling area of science.

LAYERS OF THE MIND

Psychologists often divide the mind into layers, depending on how aware, or conscious, we are of our own thoughts, feelings, or memories. There are three layers: conscious, subconscious, and unconscious.

THE CONSCIOUS MIND

Your conscious mind means the thoughts and experiences that you are aware of, and realize you are having. For example, you're using it when you talk to someone, enjoy or dislike something, notice your surroundings, learn something new, or make plans.

THE SUBCONSCIOUS MIND

Your subconscious (or "preconscious") mind is full of stuff that you're *not* thinking about, but you can if you want to—such as stored knowledge and memories. They're usually "hidden" under the surface, but you can recall them if you try.

For example, think of a family member or friend. Do you know when their birthday is? You don't normally think about it, but it's there when you need it!

MARCH 12TH!

Breathing is like this, too. It's subconscious, and you can do it without thinking. But if you want to consciously control your breathing, you can—for example, to play a wind instrument.

PARP!

Chapter 2

28

🧊 THE UNCONSCIOUS MIND

The unconscious mind contains things that are hidden from your conscious mind. That includes things like the way your brain controls your heartbeat or temperature—but also feelings or memories that are very deeply buried. They are there, but you don't realize it.

For example, maybe a zoo animal scared you when you were tiny. You can't remember it happening—but you don't like zoos, without really knowing why.

🧊 LIKE AN ICEBERG

Brain scientists often compare the layers of the mind to an iceberg that is mostly underwater.

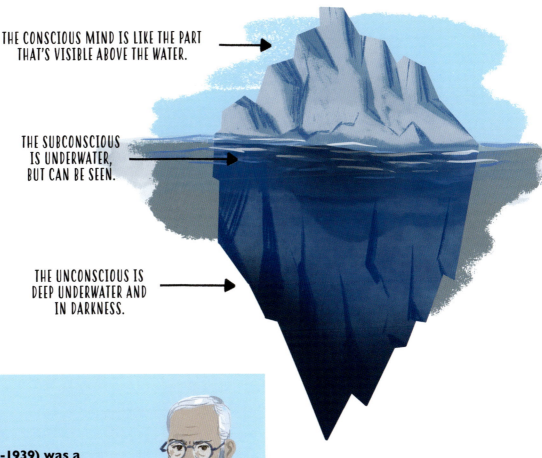

THE CONSCIOUS MIND IS LIKE THE PART THAT'S VISIBLE ABOVE THE WATER.

THE SUBCONSCIOUS IS UNDERWATER, BUT CAN BE SEEN.

THE UNCONSCIOUS IS DEEP UNDERWATER AND IN DARKNESS.

❓ SIGMUND FREUD

Sigmund Freud (1856-1939) was a famous neuroscientist and psychologist who wrote about many important brain topics, including the "layers" of the mind. He believed that the unconscious mind influences our thoughts and behaviors without us realizing it.

MEMORIES AND THE MIND

Our memories are a big part of our minds, and they affect who we are. And sometimes, our minds can trick us and make us remember things wrongly.

LINKED MEMORIES

The brain stores memories by making new connections and links, and our memories are linked together in our minds, too.

Suppose you have to name as many fruits you can in 30 seconds. It might take a while to get started—but once you think of one fruit, it triggers memories of other, similar fruits.

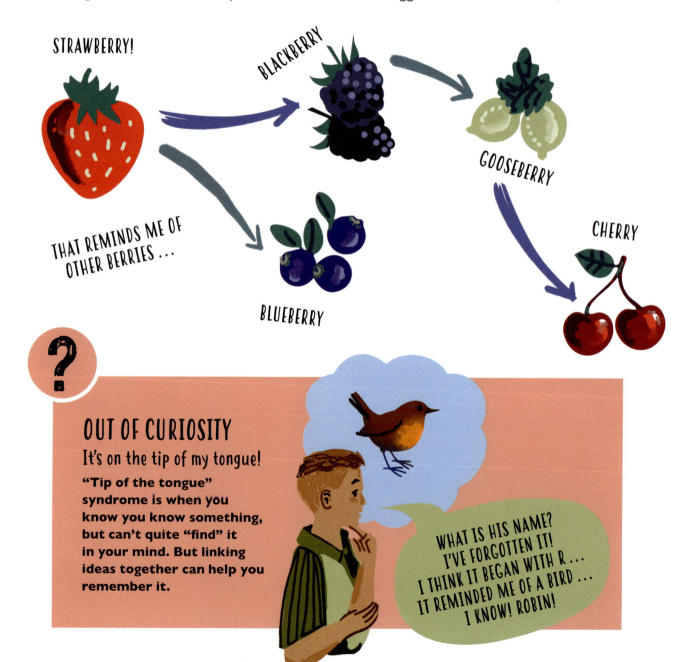

OUT OF CURIOSITY
It's on the tip of my tongue!

"Tip of the tongue" syndrome is when you know you know something, but can't quite "find" it in your mind. But linking ideas together can help you remember it.

WHAT IS HIS NAME? I'VE FORGOTTEN IT! I THINK IT BEGAN WITH R... IT REMINDED ME OF A BIRD... I KNOW! ROBIN!

SMELLS AND PLACES

When we store a new memory, we also link it to other things that are happening around us, especially the place we are in and what we can smell.

Neuroscientists think that smells are closely linked to memories because of the way the nose sends signals to the brain.

The smell-sensing cells inside the nose link directly to the limbic system, where memories are processed. So smells and other information can get stored together.

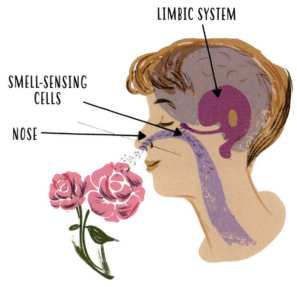

That's why a smell can trigger strong memories, even from a long time ago.

Our minds also link memories to places. So when you go back to a place or see a photo of it, other things you thought you had forgotten come flooding back.

MMMMM... THAT SMELL REMINDS ME OF MY GRANDMA'S GARDEN WHEN I WAS LITTLE!

I REMEMBER THAT VACATION! WE STAYED IN THAT COOL CAMPSITE BY THE BEACH! I LOST MY YELLOW HAT IN THE WIND! DO YOU REMEMBER THAT AMAZING ICE CREAM WE HAD?

WHEN YOU WERE A BABY, YOUR STROLLER ROLLED AWAY DOWN A HILL!

MEMORY MISTAKES

When you remember things, your brain sends signals through the same connections and pathways as when the thing really happened. Sometimes, this can cause memory mix-ups.

For example, you might read something in a book, and imagine it as if it was happening to you. Later, you "remember" it as if it was your own memory. Or people tell you about something that happened to you as a baby, and you start to feel that you remember it yourself.

Chapter 2

31

THINKING THOUGHTS

Try not to think about anything at all for 10 seconds. 3 … 2 … 1 … go!

Hard, isn't it? That's because our brains are built for thinking, and we think all the time. It's almost impossible to stop your mind from having thoughts!

TYPES OF THINKING

When we think, signals are zooming around the brain through our neuron networks. Scientists still don't know exactly how this creates thoughts, but they do know that it's very complicated. It usually involves several different parts of the brain working together, and our brains can do many different types of thinking—such as:

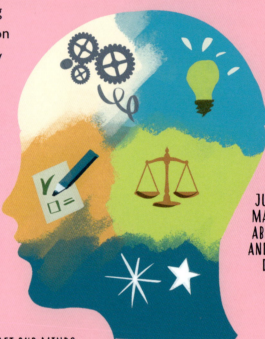

REASONING, WHERE WE FIGURE OUT IF SOMETHING MAKES SENSE

CONCEPTUALIZING, WHERE WE THINK ABOUT AN IDEA OR PLAN

JUDGING AND DECISION-MAKING, WHERE WE THINK ABOUT DIFFERENT OPTIONS AND WHAT THEY MEAN, AND DECIDE WHICH IS BEST

PROBLEM-SOLVING, WHERE WE TRY TO THINK OF A SOLUTION OR ANSWER TO A PROBLEM

DAYDREAMING, WHERE WE LET OUR MINDS WANDER AND IMAGINE THINGS, OR GO OVER SOMETHING THAT HAPPENED

FAST AND SLOW

You can think quickly and automatically, like when you're playing a sport or chatting and laughing with friends. Your brain is busy, but you don't think about each individual thought, and can react quickly.

You can also think more slowly and deliberately, like when you're trying to do a hard puzzle, or understand an explanation. You can feel yourself concentrating and focusing on that one thing.

DO WE THINK IN WORDS?

Some psychologists believe that we mainly use language to think, with words creating our ideas. You can even have a kind of silent "voice" inside your head as you think thoughts to yourself.

If words didn't exist, would you still be able to think in the same way? Others argue that you can think without language. In a daydream, you might just imagine a series of events in your "mind's eye." Or an artist might think of a picture or sculpture they want to create as a visual image.

IS THE BRAIN A COMPUTER?

Computers store information and do calculations by sending electrical signals along pathways and connections in electronic circuits.

Since electronic computers were invented in the 1930s and 40s, neuroscientists have realized that the brain works in a similar way. But the brain is more complicated and has emotions and consciousness—so we can't say that it's exactly like a computer.

THE NETWORK OF MICROSCOPIC CIRCUITS IN A COMPUTER CHIP ARE A BIT LIKE THE NEURON NETWORKS IN THE BRAIN.

OUT OF CURIOSITY
Many ways of thinking

In fact, we probably all think in several different ways, and people think differently from each other. Some think more in words, others more in pictures. It depends on who you are and what you're thinking about.

Chapter 2

33

PERCEPTION

Perception is how we experience the world and what's happening around us. It's not just about what our senses take in, but about how the mind interprets the information.

👁 MEMORY-MATCHING

When your brain receives signals from your senses, it compares them to things stored in its memory. That's how you recognize what you are seeing, hearing, or sensing.

For example, you might have never see these pictures before, but you can recognize what they are.

YOU KNOW THAT THIS IS A FACE, BECAUSE IT HAS THE SAME PARTS AND BASIC SHAPE AS ALL THE OTHER FACES YOU'VE SEEN.

👁 MATCHING MIX-UPS

Sometimes you'll have a moment of confusion when your brain isn't sure what it's experiencing and tries to match it to the wrong memory. This happens when you think you see someone you know, but it's actually someone else who looks a little bit like them.

HEY... THAT'S UNCLE ALEX! OH, NO IT'S NOT! OOPS!

👁 DUCK OR RABBIT?

The famous duck and rabbit illusion helps to show how perception works.

Do you see a duck or a rabbit?

THE PICTURE IS DESIGNED SO THAT YOUR MIND CAN SEE IT AS A DUCK OR A RABBIT. MOST PEOPLE CAN SEE THEM BOTH, BUT IT'S VERY HARD TO MAKE YOUR MIND SEE BOTH AT THE SAME TIME. IT WANTS TO "MATCH" THE PICTURE TO ONE MEMORY OR THE OTHER.

👁 STRETCHY TIME

Seconds, minutes, and hours always tick by at the same speed—but our minds can perceive time very differently in different situations. When you're bored or waiting for something, time seems to slow down. When you're busy or having a good time, it seems to go faster!

Scientists think that this is because when your mind is busier and has more inputs, it interprets that as more time going by.

OUT OF CURIOSITY
Seeing things

Our minds try so hard to do this "matching" that we also "recognize" familiar things, especially faces, in random objects or patterns—an effect called pareidolia.

WE OFTEN SEE FACES IN HOUSES... CARS... OR EVEN RANDOM ROCKS, LIKE THIS ONE ON MARS.

Chapter 2

35

EMOTIONS

You've probably had quite a few emotions already today. Happiness, love, anger, jealousy, or maybe feeling annoyed, excited, or bored.

WHAT ARE EMOTIONS?

We're all familiar with emotions—most of us have a wide range of them every day. But they are actually quite complicated, since they affect you in several ways at the same time. Imagine you're going to perform on stage and feel REALLY nervous.

In your mind …
You're thinking about how you feel.

In your body …
You get a fluttery "butterflies in your stomach" feeling, your heart beats faster, or you might even feel sick.

In your expression …
The nervousness affects your face, voice, and body language. You look worried and hunched up, and your voice sounds wobbly.

OH NO, I WISH I HADN'T AGREED TO DO THIS! EVERYONE WILL BE LOOKING AT ME - WHAT IF I MESS UP?

THUMP! THUMP! THUMP! FLUTTER!

I CAN'T… I'M TOO NERVOUS!

Chapter 2

36

😨😊 MANAGING EMOTIONS

You can sometimes manage your emotions, and overcome them. You might be really upset or scared, but you can calm yourself down after a while. This is hard for small children, but as we grow up, we learn to manage, or "regulate," our emotions and not always act on them. Often, other people can help with that, too.

YOU CAN DO IT – DON'T WORRY, YOU'LL BE FINE!

😨😊 WHAT ARE EMOTIONS FOR?

Emotions are reactions to things happening around you that prepare you for action and show others what's happening, too. So, for example, fear is a reaction to your brain thinking you're in danger. It sends signals to your body to speed up your heartbeat so you can fight or run if you need to. And your face or voice warns other people of the danger. We evolved these reactions to help us survive and live together in groups.

UUGGH, HELP!

EVERYONE'S EMOTIONS

Psychologists think there are a few basic emotions that all humans share. They've found that people from all over the world seem to have these same emotions and express them in the same ways. This suggests that they are instinctive, or built in to our brains, and not something we learn. They include:

HAPPINESS OR JOY
DISGUST
FEAR
ANGER
SADNESS
SURPRISE

Chapter 2

37

PERSONALITY

 Personality means what you're like—your character, the way you think and behave, your likes and dislikes, and how you do things. Each person's personality is unique and made of many different aspects.

WHAT DECIDES PERSONALITY?

Like many things, your personality is influenced by things you're born with and things you experienced—often described as "nature and nurture."

For example, Kai hates dancing—but why?

It could be because he's naturally not very musical and finds it difficult and annoying.

Or maybe someone laughed at his dancing one time, and now he's too scared to try.

Or maybe both! Everyone's personality is a big mixture of things with lots of different causes, and you might not even know what some of them are.

A person's personality can sometimes change over time, too. For example, Kai might see other people having fun dancing and decide to try it after all. Then he might end up enjoying it and become a great dancer!

Chapter 2

38

MEASURING PERSONALITY

Psychologists have come up with several systems to classify and measure different personality traits, or qualities. Here's one of them, known as the "Five Factor" or "Big Five" system. It measures five traits, each on a sliding scale.

FRIENDLY, EAGER TO PLEASE	**AGREEABLENESS**	LESS BOTHERED BY WHAT OTHERS THINK
EXTROVERT—LOVES BEING AROUND OTHER PEOPLE	**EXTROVERT OR INTROVERT?**	INTROVERT—NEEDS LOTS OF TIME ALONE
LIKES NEW EXPERIENCES, CURIOUS	**OPENNESS**	LIKES ROUTINE AND FAMILIARITY
EASILY STRESSED, A WORRIER	**NEUROTICISM**	RELAXED AND CALM
ORGANIZED AND STICKS TO RULES	**CONSCIENTIOUSNESS**	SCATTY, UNTIDY, OR ALWAYS LATE

TAKE A LOOK, AND SEE WHERE YOU THINK YOU WOULD PUT YOURSELF ON THE SCALE FOR EACH ONE.

WHAT DO YOU SEE?

Another way to measure personality is to test how people react to or understand things. In the twentieth century, two different psychologists, Hermann Rorschach in the 1920s and Wayne Holtzman in the 1960s, developed "inkblot" tests. What you see in a random pattern of lines or blots can reveal how you think and relate to the world.

For example, what does this inkblot make you think of?

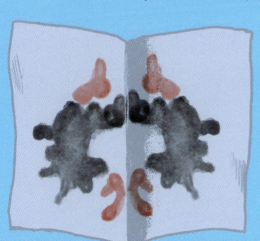

A HELPFUL, FRIENDLY EXTROVERT MIGHT SEE TWO PEOPLE WORKING TOGETHER.

SOMEONE WHO'S EASILY WORRIED OR STRESSED MIGHT SEE A SCARY FACE.

Chapter 2

39

INTELLIGENCE

Intelligence means how clever or smart you are. It's an idea we all know and talk about, yet it's actually quite hard for psychologists to say exactly what it is or to measure it.

SIGNS OF INTELLIGENCE

Most psychologists say intelligence is made up of a group of abilities that use brain power. They usually include:

 Identifying and solving problems

 Learning from experience

 Reasoning, or understanding logic, cause, and effect

 Analysing, or finding patterns and meaning in information

 Innovating, or coming up with new ideas.

WHAT IS IQ?

IQ stands for "Intelligence Quotient," or intelligence level. It's a way of giving each person an intelligence "score." You can show the range of different people's IQs on a graph, like this:

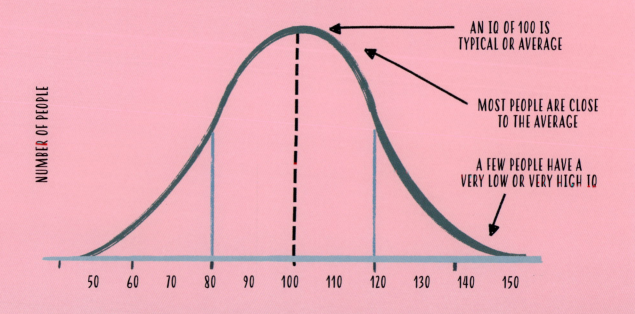

AN IQ OF 100 IS TYPICAL OR AVERAGE

MOST PEOPLE ARE CLOSE TO THE AVERAGE

A FEW PEOPLE HAVE A VERY LOW OR VERY HIGH IQ

INTELLIGENCE TESTS

An intelligence test, or IQ test, is kind of quiz with questions and puzzles to test your intelligence. The questions are things like:

1 WHICH IS THE ODD ONE OUT?

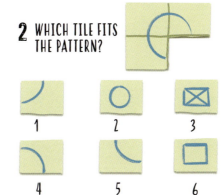

2 WHICH TILE FITS THE PATTERN?

3 IF FORK GOES WITH FOOD, WHICH OF THESE GOES WITH SAND?

TESTING PROBLEMS

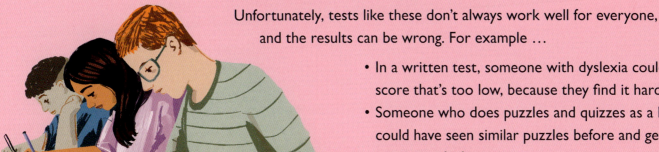

Unfortunately, tests like these don't always work well for everyone, and the results can be wrong. For example …

- In a written test, someone with dyslexia could get a score that's too low, because they find it hard to read.
- Someone who does puzzles and quizzes as a hobby could have seen similar puzzles before and get an inaccurate high score.
- Or what if you're anxious and hate tests? You could get a low score just because you're so stressed.

TYPES OF INTELLIGENCE

Psychologists now recognize that there are other types of intelligence too, besides IQ. Here are some of them …

- EQ or emotional intelligence—understanding other people and emotions
- Crystallized intelligence—knowledge and wisdom gained over a long time
- Kinesthetic intelligence—control over your body, quick reactions, and timing
- Visuospatial intelligence—thinking in images and understanding how things fit together.

IQ TEST ANSWERS

1 = THE TELESCOPE, SINCE IT'S THE ONLY ONE THAT DOESN'T MEASURE SOMETHING.
2 = 1
3 = SPADE

Chapter 2

41

NEURODIVERSITY

As well as having different personalities, our minds all work in slightly different ways, thanks to differences in our neurons and brain structure. These differences are known as neurodiversity.

∞ BRAIN "WIRING"

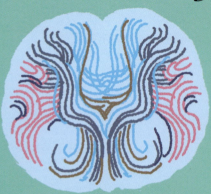

Our neurons make new connections when we experience, learn, and remember things. But they also have a basic set of connections, or "wiring" that the brain uses to do things like process sense signals and control the body.

Our brain wiring is mainly passed on from our parents in our genes and DNA (see page 66), and just like the rest of your body, it varies from one person to another.

∞ BUILT-IN DIFFERENCES

Being musical, having a good memory, and finding mental arithmetic easy, are all things that are thought to be affected by our brain wiring. You can learn these things and get better at them, but some people naturally find them easier.

MUSICAL ABILITY SEEMS TO BE BUILT INTO OUR BRAINS AND PASSED DOWN IN FAMILIES.

IT MAKES IT EASIER TO UNDERSTAND AND COPY TUNES AND RHYTHMS, AND LEARN TO PLAY INSTRUMENTS.

Meanwhile, some people have a different condition, amusia, that makes them unable to process or enjoy music.

IT JUST SOUNDS LIKE RANDOM NOISES!

Chapter 2

42

∞ NEURODIVERGENT CONDITIONS

Some people have brain wiring that can make particular tasks or situations unusually difficult—or sometimes extra easy—or it can affect how they experience things. They are sometimes diagnosed with "neurodivergent" conditions, such as:

AUTISM
Can make it hard to understand other people's feelings, expressions, or social "rules"—but autistic people are sometimes very good at other things such as art, mathematics, or computing.

ADHD
Makes it difficult to concentrate, get organized or stay still or calm. Often, goes with being creative, caring, or sociable.

DYSLEXIA
Makes reading, writing, and spelling extra difficult to learn. Dyslexic people often have strong visuospatial intelligence (see page 41).

DYSPRAXIA
In dyspraxia, the neuron signals that control your body can be slowed down or blocked, making things like tying shoelaces or riding a bike hard to learn.

OUT OF CURIOSITY
Mixed-up senses
About 2–4% of people have an unusual neurodivergent condition called synesthesia, meaning "together-senses." They have extra connections in the brain that can make one sensation trigger another. For example, you might see colors or feel textures when you hear sounds or smell something. Many people also see colors for different numbers, letters, days, or months.

SOME ARTISTS USE THEIR SYNESTHESIA TO INSPIRE THEIR WORK.

Chapter 2

43

CHAPTER 3

HUMAN BEHAVIOR

The brain and the mind don't just run our bodies and control our inner thoughts. They are also in charge of how we behave, how we understand ourselves, and how we communicate and interact with other people.

In this chapter, we'll explore the science of the self and others. How do you build a picture of yourself as an individual person? How do people influence each other's behavior, and why do we sometimes make bad decisions? And how is it that as well as other people, we have such close friendships with other species, such as dogs? This fascinating area is a vital part of psychology and brain science.

ANCIENT IDEAS

Long before psychology and brain science officially existed, philosophers, poets, politicians, and religious leaders studied and wrote about human behavior. They often noticed the same kinds of things that psychologists study today.

WHAT PEOPLE ARE LIKE

Sometimes they simply observed and described human behavior. Sei Shōnagon was a Japanese poet and diary writer who lived in the 900s. She worked as a lady-in-waiting to the Empress of Japan and often described the behavior, quirks, and annoying habits of people she knew and observed.

"A MAN WHO HAS NOTHING IN PARTICULAR TO RECOMMEND HIM DISCUSSES ALL SORTS OF SUBJECTS AT RANDOM AS IF HE KNEW EVERYTHING."

HOW TO BE HAPPY

"VERY LITTLE IS NEEDED TO MAKE A HAPPY LIFE; IT IS ALL WITHIN YOURSELF, IN YOUR WAY OF THINKING".

Many ancient thinkers and writers observed how anger, bitterness, and jealousy could make people unhappy.

Ancient Roman emperor Marcus Aurelius is famous for his writings on goodness and happiness. He believed that changing how you think about things can make you happier.

Chapter 3

46

THE FOUR HUMORS

The ancient Greeks believed that the body contained four humors, or fluids: blood, yellow bile, black bile, and phlegm. They thought that illnesses were caused by the humors being unbalanced. This belief lasted for over 1,000 years, until the 1700s.

Each humour also represented a different personality trait—so different kinds of personality and behavior could be explained by having too much, or too little, of a particular humour.

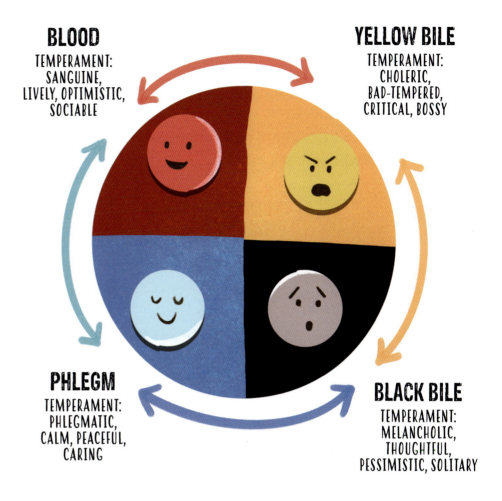

BLOOD
TEMPERAMENT: SANGUINE, LIVELY, OPTIMISTIC, SOCIABLE

YELLOW BILE
TEMPERAMENT: CHOLERIC, BAD-TEMPERED, CRITICAL, BOSSY

PHLEGM
TEMPERAMENT: PHLEGMATIC, CALM, PEACEFUL, CARING

BLACK BILE
TEMPERAMENT: MELANCHOLIC, THOUGHTFUL, PESSIMISTIC, SOLITARY

THE THREE DOSHAS

Ancient Indian traditional medicine, known as Ayurveda, has a similar system called the three doshas. Everyone is said to have their own mixture of the three, which decides their temperament and behavior.

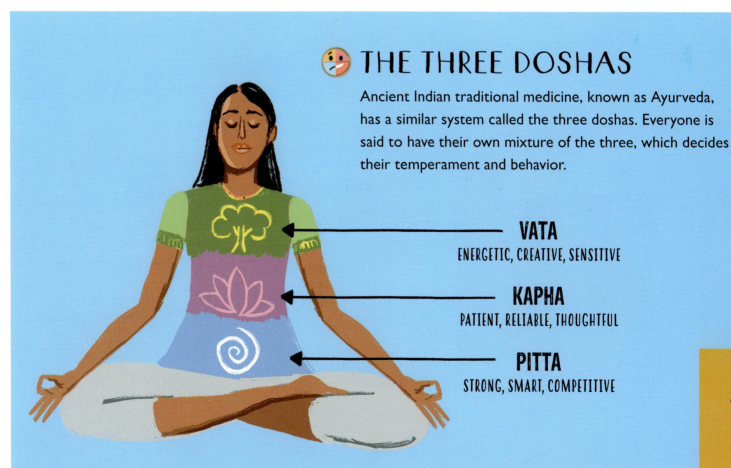

VATA
ENERGETIC, CREATIVE, SENSITIVE

KAPHA
PATIENT, RELIABLE, THOUGHTFUL

PITTA
STRONG, SMART, COMPETITIVE

WHO AM I?

We can all think to ourselves inside our own minds, and that gives us a sense of "self," or "self-image." It means your idea of who you are and your relationships with other people.

As the famous French scientist and writer René Descartes said in 1637 …

"I THINK, THEREFORE I AM."

WHO AM I TO OTHERS?

Most people feel a need to belong to groups and spend time with other people. We get a sense of who we are partly through our relationships with others.

In other words, if you can think about your own existence, that must mean you exist and have a self!

I'M MY MOTHER AND FATHER'S DAUGHTER …

ALI'S SISTER …

ONE OF MS LIN'S PUPILS …

I'M MAYA.

AND SCRUFFY'S HUMAN!

Chapter 3

48

👀 GETTING FEEDBACK

Others reflect back at us how they feel about us, too, and that adds to your sense of self. For example, your friends, parents, or teacher might tell you that you're brave, funny, a worrier, good at drawing, or maybe that you talk too much! It all goes into your brain's memory banks and adds to your self-image.

Your own experiences and feelings about yourself are important, too. How you feel about yourself can grow and change as you do new things.

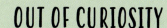

OUT OF CURIOSITY
Dunbar's number

British psychologist Robin Dunbar studies human relationships and friendships. He found that most people have "circles" of relationships, with fewer people in the closest circles. Overall, most people know about 150 others, though they can recognize many more.

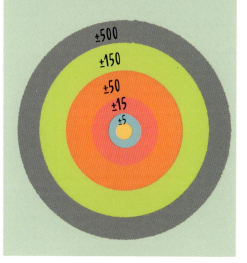

👀 SELF-AWARENESS

Self-awareness means having a good understanding of your own personality and behavior. Sometimes, we can be wrong about ourselves! For example, if you're a perfectionist, you might think you're not good enough if you don't always do things perfectly.

Chapter 3

49

SPEECH AND LANGUAGE

As you read these words, their meaning and the ideas they contain go into your brain! That's an amazing thing that no other living thing can do—only humans.

WORDS AND RULES

Some animals do use different sounds to mean different things. For example, a blackbird has an alarm call to warn other birds of danger …

… which is very different from its tuneful mating song.

But human language is much more complex. As well as each person having thousands of words stored in their brain, our languages have rules, or grammar, that we use to arrange words into sentences. So we can put words together to say pretty much anything we like.

LANGUAGE IN THE BRAIN

No one knows exactly when humans first developed language, but it was probably at least 100,000 years ago. We have special brain areas, Broca's area and Wernicke's area (see page 11) that help us to understand and create speech. Our mouths and tongues have also evolved to make a wide range of different speech sounds.

- LIPS
- TEETH
- TONGUE
- VOCAL CORDS

WE USE ALL THESE PARTS TO MAKE THE SOUNDS OF DIFFERENT WORDS.

Scientists have found that different languages all over the world all have similarities, such as nouns and verbs, grammar rules, and syllables. This could mean that the way language works is "wired" into the human brain and is the same in everyone.

ITALIAN, SPOKEN IN ITALY AND SWITZERLAND, EUROPE

LAO, SPOKEN IN LAOS, ASIA

QUECHUA, SPOKEN IN THE ANDES IN SOUTH AMERICA

ENGLISH, SPOKEN IN MANY PARTS OF THE WORLD

SHARING IDEAS

Language is incredibly useful. We can use it to share knowledge and ideas, and store them in books, so they can be passed down through time.

SOCIAL LANGUAGE

We also use language in a social way—to show friendship, make each other laugh, or express ourselves in poems, stories, and songs.

FAMILIAR PHRASES LIKE THIS ARE A WAY OF SAYING "WE'RE FRIENDS."

SHARING A SPORTS CHANT OR SONG HELPS PEOPLE FEEL PART OF A GROUP.

Chapter 3

51

NONVERBAL COMMUNICATION

Nonverbal means "without words." As well as using language, we send each other lots of signals and messages in other ways, using our faces and bodies.

FACIAL EXPRESSIONS

Some facial expressions express basic emotions that any other human can understand (see page 37). But we can make much more complex facial expressions, too.

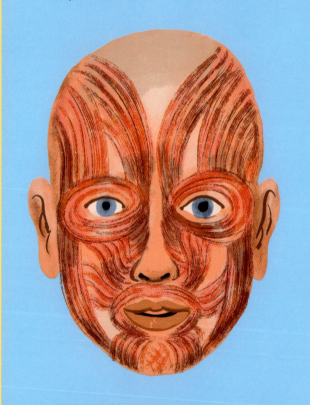

WE HAVE 43 MUSCLES IN OUR FACES, JUST UNDER THE SKIN, WHICH WE CAN MOVE TO MAKE LOTS OF DIFFERENT EXPRESSIONS.

10,000 FACES

The American psychologist Paul Ekman, an expert in facial expressions, discovered that we can make up to 10,000 of them. They can show all kinds of information—and most people are also good at "reading" them to understand what other people are thinking.

THAT'S A LITTLE ANNOYING, BUT NEVER MIND!

STOP SHINING THAT FLASHLIGHT IN MY EYES!

OH FOR GOODNESS' SAKE, NOT AGAIN!

YEAH, RIGHT. I DON'T BELIEVE YOU.

In fact, facial expressions can sometimes reveal how we really feel, even if it's different to what we're saying. We can also make "micro-expressions"—very quick, instant expressions that reveal our true thoughts, even if we're trying to hide them.

Chapter 3

52

👋 BODY LANGUAGE

We also use our bodies to communicate with gestures and movements. Some of these are different in different societies or different parts of the world, and we learn them as we grow up.

WAVING GETS PEOPLE'S ATTENTION.

POINTING SHOWS SOMEONE ELSE WHERE TO LOOK, TO SEE WHAT YOU'RE SEEING.

CLAPPING SAYS "YAY! WELL DONE!"

NODDING OR SHAKING YOUR HEAD CAN MEAN YES OR NO.

OUT OF CURIOSITY
Programming your brain

Facial expressions and body language can express our feelings or thoughts—but they can also work in reverse. For example, if you make yourself smile, it can help to cheer you up. If you're nervous, standing in a strong, upright position can help you feel braver and more positive.

THIS COULD BE BECAUSE OUR BRAINS EXPECT OUR FEELINGS TO MATCH WHAT OUR FACES AND BODIES ARE DOING.

Chapter 3

GROUPS

Humans have evolved to do things together in groups. Studying how we behave in groups, and how they affect us, is an important area of psychology and brain science.

GROUPS ARE EVERYWHERE!

Groups exist at every level of society. They can give people support, help their members to survive, or use teamwork to get things done. And the groups you belong to can be an important part of your sense of self. Even if you're an introvert who likes being alone (see page 39), you're probably a member of several groups.

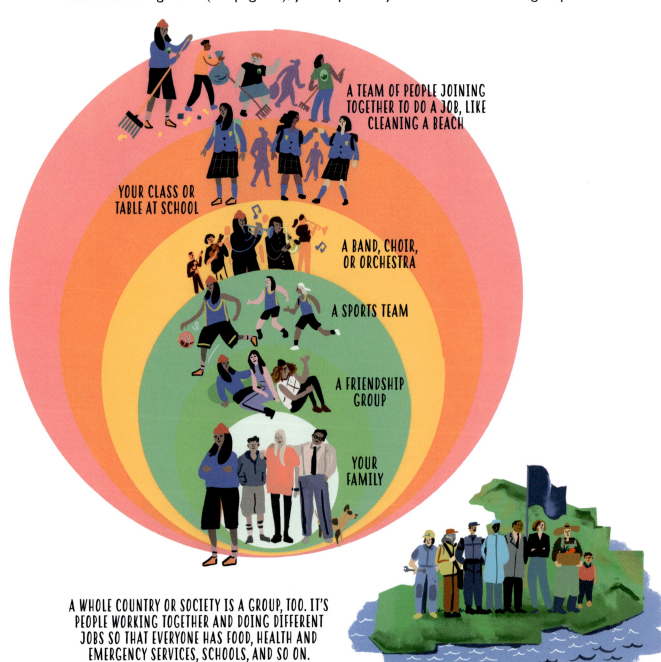

A TEAM OF PEOPLE JOINING TOGETHER TO DO A JOB, LIKE CLEANING A BEACH

YOUR CLASS OR TABLE AT SCHOOL

A BAND, CHOIR, OR ORCHESTRA

A SPORTS TEAM

A FRIENDSHIP GROUP

YOUR FAMILY

A WHOLE COUNTRY OR SOCIETY IS A GROUP, TOO. IT'S PEOPLE WORKING TOGETHER AND DOING DIFFERENT JOBS SO THAT EVERYONE HAS FOOD, HEALTH AND EMERGENCY SERVICES, SCHOOLS, AND SO ON.

ROLES IN GROUPS

Psychologists have found that the members of a group usually take on different roles. Roles can be decided by several things:

- Abilities, skills, and personality. Some people make good leaders. Some are more reserved, but have other skills like organizing things. Or you might be the "joker" who makes everyone laugh.
- How long you've been in the group—for example, the leader is usually someone who's been there for longer.
- What the group needs. A band needs a variety of instruments, and that decides who can join and what each person does.

THINK OF A GROUP YOU'RE IN, LIKE A GROUP OF FRIENDS OR A SCHOOL CLASS. DO PEOPLE TAKE ON DIFFERENT ROLES—SUCH AS LEADER, JOKER, PEACEMAKER, ORGANIZER, OR THE THINKER WHO ALWAYS COMES UP WITH NEW IDEAS? HOW WOULD YOU DESCRIBE YOUR ROLE?

US AND THEM

Sometimes, people are so loyal to a group that they can start to see other groups as enemies. It can happen with cliques in a school, for example, or fans of different sports teams. Psychologists call this tribalism. Sometimes it's friendly and harmless, but at its worst, tribalism can lead to bullying, fighting, or even wars.

INFLUENCING EACH OTHER

Have you ever done something you didn't really want to do, just because everyone else was? You're not alone! Human behavior is strongly influenced by other people.

FITTING IN

Though everyone is different, most people want to feel accepted by others, since it's human nature to do things with other people. When you're in a group—whether that's a group of friends, a drama club or a whole country—there are expectations about how you should behave, known as "norms."

If you fit in with the group's norms, you'll feel accepted or even be praised. This triggers parts of the brain known as the "reward system," which makes you feel good and want to keep doing the same thing.

But if you don't fit in, others in the group might disapprove or judge you harshly. Psychologists call this "stigma." They could even ostracize you, or leave you out. That feels horrible, so most people try to avoid it.

GROUPTHINK

Trying to fit in can lead to something called "groupthink," where people are so anxious about being left out or judged, that they always go along with what they think everyone else thinks! This can become more important than making sensible decisions or asking questions.

This means that people often behave differently in a group than they would on their own. That isn't always bad—for example, a group could work together to rescue someone. But sometimes, it leads to harmful or dangerous behavior.

PREJUDICES AND STEREOTYPES

Humans also tend to classify other people into groups, or types, and make judgements about them. A prejudice is when you assume something about someone without knowing them.

A STEREOTYPE IS A FIXED IDEA ABOUT WHAT A PARTICULAR GROUP OF PEOPLE IS LIKE.

Attitudes like this can influence people and make them feel that they shouldn't do things that people don't expect them to. It can be hard to stand up to stereotypes and prejudice and do your own thing.

Chapter 3

57

MAKING MISTAKES

We might have the most powerful brains on the planet, but sometimes, our brains make mistakes, or decisions that don't make much sense.

⚠️ LOOKING FOR PATTERNS

Human brains are always searching for patterns and connections. This is extremely useful, since it helps us understand how things work and learn what to expect.

For example, you might notice that when there are dark clouds in the sky, it often rains soon afterward. And it's true—clouds do lead to rain.

⚠️ IT'S AN ILLUSION!

However, our brains are so ready to spot patterns, we can also see links where there aren't any. This is called "illusory correlation"—meaning that something looks like a link, but isn't.

For example, what if someone fails two spelling tests, both on a Monday. They might decide it's because Mondays are bad luck. In fact, their test results have nothing to do with what day it is!

⚠ CONFIRMATION BIAS

Once we get an idea in our heads—such as "Mondays are bad luck"—we can then start looking for evidence for it.

But we're more likely to *ignore* evidence that doesn't match our beliefs. The same person might win a prize on a Monday, but not notice that this is actually good luck and goes against their theory.

This is called "confirmation bias," and it can lead to unwise decisions. In this case, someone might avoid doing things on Mondays and miss out on all kinds of opportunities—all for no good reason!

OUT OF CURIOSITY
What a bargain!

Have you ever wondered why stores often give items prices like $5.99 or $99.99? Even though $5.99 is almost the same as $6, our brains are more likely to remember the figure 5 and perceive the price as cheaper.

Chapter 3

ANIMALS AND US

Our brains and minds help us communicate with other people, understand their facial expressions, and care about what others think. But can we do this with animals, too?

LIVING TOGETHER

There are many different species of animals, and some are very unlike us. It's hard to make friends with a fly or a jellyfish.

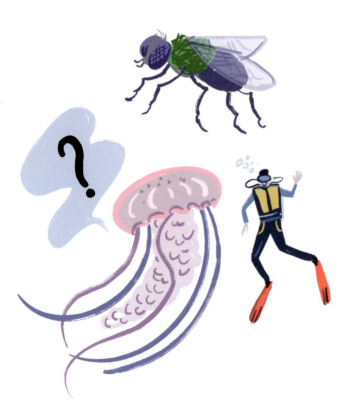

But other animals, such as dogs, cats, and horses, can be our pets or working companions. We've been living alongside them or training them for thousands of years. In some cases, humans and animals have evolved to understand each other.

BEST FRIENDS

This is especially true for dogs. Pet dogs don't exist in the wild. They evolved when humans began training and breeding wild wolves, turning them into pets and helpers. Psychologists and neuroscientists have studied dog brains and behavior, and found that they have evolved to understand our faces and voices, and to make facial expressions that humans can understand, too.

DOGS CAN SHOW THOUGHTS AND FEELINGS WITH THEIR FACES, LIKE WE CAN. CAN YOU IDENTIFY THESE DOG EXPRESSIONS?

Chapter 3

60

BIRD BRAINS

Dogs are mammals like us. Birds belong to a different animal group, but some of them are very intelligent and can learn human words. A few, such as parrots and crows, can "make friends" with humans and recognize individual people.

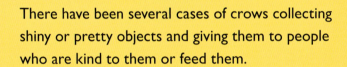

There have been several cases of crows collecting shiny or pretty objects and giving them to people who are kind to them or feed them.

Alex the parrot was an African gray parrot who learned over 100 words and could have simple conversations with the scientist who worked with him, Irene Pepperberg.

INSTINCTIVE FEARS

Meanwhile, some animals can be dangerous to humans. By studying babies, psychologists have found that fear of spiders and snakes is a natural instinct, which has become built in to our brains as we have evolved. In prehistoric times, avoiding these animals would have helped us to survive, since they can have a venomous bite.

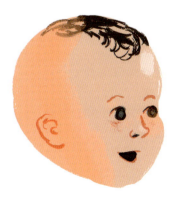  

THE SCIENTISTS FOUND THAT BABIES WERE ALARMED BY PICTURES OF SNAKES AND SPIDERS, BUT NOT BY OTHER ANIMALS OR PLANTS—EVEN IF THEY HAD NEVER SEEN A SNAKE OR SPIDER BEFORE.

CHAPTER 4

GROWING AND CHANGING

Your brain and your mind change throughout your life, starting from long before birth. As we are born and grow up, the brain develops and grows countless connections, and our minds, memories, personalities, and abilities take shape.

How do newborn babies make sense of the world around them? How do children learn to talk, read, think, make decisions, and understand other people? Why does the brain go through a time of turmoil when you're a teenager, and when do the brain and mind "grow up"? And what happens as the brain grows old? We'll find out in this chapter.

HOW THE BRAIN EVOLVED

Humans have powerful, complex brains that change, grow, and learn throughout our lives. But how did this happen? Like other body parts, our brains have evolved, or developed over many generations.

HOW BRAINS BEGAN

Life on Earth began around 4 billion (4,000,000,000) years ago. Early living things were single-celled, similar to bacteria, and had no brains. Gradually, they evolved into more complex living things. Scientists think the first brains evolved around 550 million years ago in simple wormlike creatures.

THE FIRST LIVING THINGS WERE MICROSCOPIC AND TOO SIMPLE TO HAVE BRAINS.

FLATWORMS LIKE THIS WERE AMONG THE EARLIEST ANIMALS WITH BRAINS.

EVOLUTIONARY PSYCHOLOGY

For most of human history, we lived a much wilder life. We had to forage or hunt for food and deal with dangerous wild animals. Most people have a different lifestyle now, but our brains haven't changed as much. Evolutionary psychologists study how this could explain some kinds of thinking and behavior.

For example, lots of people are afraid of the dark, even when they're safe. We probably evolved to fear darkness because early humans slept outdoors and could have been attacked by wild animals.

HANDY HUMANS

Over the next 500 million years, animals evolved into many new and different forms, from worms, fish, and insects to dinosaurs, whales, and apes. About 4 millions years ago, some tree-dwelling apes moved down from the trees and began spending more time on land. They evolved into the earliest humans, known as *Homo habilis* or "handy human," which evolved into other human species.

WALKING UPRIGHT ON TWO LEGS LET HUMANS USE THEIR HANDS MORE—FOR EXAMPLE, TO MAKE STONE TOOLS.

HOMO HABILIS

HOMO ERECTUS

LATER HUMANS LEARNED TO USE FIRE TO COOK. COOKING MEAT MADE IT EASIER TO EAT AND DIGEST, GIVING HUMANS MORE ENERGY, AND THIS HELPED OUR BRAINS GROW BIGGER AND SMARTER.

HOMO HEIDELBERGENSIS

SOME EARLY HUMAN SPECIES BEGAN BUILDING SHELTERS, TOO.

SMART HUMANS

Today, there's only one human species left. That's us, modern humans, known as *Homo sapiens* ("smart human"). Our brains do a lot of developing and growing after we're born, and it takes a long time to become an adult—so human parents have to care for and look after their children for many years.

NATURE AND NURTURE

Psychologists and brain scientists often talk about "nature and nurture." They are the two main factors that control how our brains and minds grow and change. So what are they?

🧬 NATURE

Nature means our DNA, a chemical found in our cells. It contains genes that tell cells how to do their jobs. Genes and DNA are passed on from parents in the cells that make babies, and they control how we grow and how our bodies work.

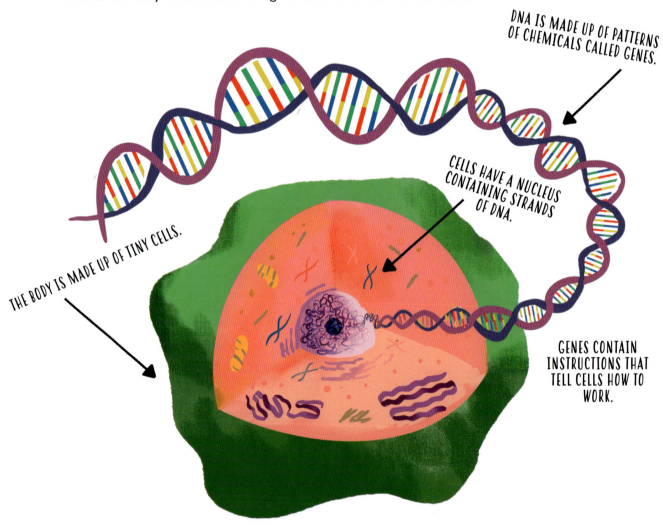

DNA IS MADE UP OF PATTERNS OF CHEMICALS CALLED GENES.

CELLS HAVE A NUCLEUS CONTAINING STRANDS OF DNA.

THE BODY IS MADE UP OF TINY CELLS.

GENES CONTAIN INSTRUCTIONS THAT TELL CELLS HOW TO WORK.

Things decided mainly by nature include:
- The basic structure of the brain, nervous system, and sense organs
- "Brain wiring" abilities or conditions, like dyslexia or natural musical ability
- Eye color, skin color, and other physical features

🧬 NURTURE

Nurture means experiences and things that happen to you. They can affect your brain, mind, and personality, including the way the brain grows and works.

Nurture includes things like:
- How you are brought up and cared for
- Experiences, sensations, and things you learn and remember
- Your diet, surroundings, and environmental factors such as pollution.

THE WORD *NURTURE* ACTUALLY MEANS CARING, FEEDING, AND LOOKING AFTER SOMEONE, WHICH HUMAN PARENTS OR CARERS DO FOR THEIR CHILDREN.

🧬 A MIXTURE OF BOTH

Many things are a mixture of nature and nurture. For example, your height is mostly decided by genes and DNA, and being taller or shorter runs in families. But your diet, and some types of diseases and medicines, can also affect how tall you end up being.

🧬 WHICH IS WHICH?

Sometimes, it's very hard to tell whether something is caused by nature or nurture, or which is more important.

For example, a child might learn to read unusually early. Is that because their brain is naturally wired to find reading easy? Or is it more down to people reading to them from a young age and giving them lots of books? Scientists often aren't sure, and sometimes they do experiments (see page 80) to try and untangle questions like these.

Chapter 4

67

BABY BRAINS

You have a brain long before you're born! It takes about nine months for a baby to grow in the womb, and the brain is growing for most of that time.

4 WEEKS (1 MONTH)
BY ABOUT FOUR WEEKS, THE EMBRYO, OR EARLY UNBORN BABY, GROWS A PART CALLED THE NEURAL TUBE, WHICH WILL BECOME THE BRAIN AND SPINE.

3 MONTHS
BY THREE MONTHS, THE BRAIN HAS FORMED DIFFERENT PARTS.

5 MONTHS
BY FIVE MONTHS, THE BRAIN HAS GROWN BILLIONS OF NEURONS.

7 MONTHS
EVEN BEFORE BIRTH, BABIES START LEARNING AND REMEMBERING THINGS, SUCH AS THE SOUNDS OF SONGS AND VOICES THEY CAN HEAR.

9 MONTHS
THE BABY IS READY TO BE BORN.

INTO THE WORLD

When a baby is born, it already has almost as many neurons in its brain as an adult does, but many fewer connections. All the things a newborn baby experiences start to build more and more connections.

COLORS, SHAPES, AND PATTERNS

MUSIC, LAUGHTER, AND OTHER SOUNDS—INCLUDING THE BABY'S OWN CRYING, GURGLING, OR BABBLING

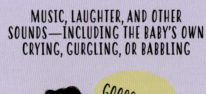

THE SENSATION OF MOVING ITS OWN BODY PARTS AND TRYING TO CONTROL THEM

BEING CUDDLED AND THE FEELING OF CLOTHES, TOYS, AND OTHER OBJECTS

LOVING CARE

To help their brains develop, babies need lots of love and affection. When parents or carers talk to babies, hold them, and respond when they cry, it helps the limbic system—which deals with strong emotions—to grow and connect to other parts of the brain.

To help this happen, both babies and adults have evolved to be drawn toward each other, and especially to each other's faces.

NEWBORN BABIES ARE INTERESTED IN HUMAN FACES, AND THEY LEARN TO RECOGNIZE THE FACE OF THEIR MAIN CARER.

MEANWHILE, ADULTS HAVE A NATURAL INSTINCT TO CARE FOR BABIES. THE WAY A BABY LOOKS AND SOUNDS TRIGGERS A CARING, LOVING RESPONSE.

OUT OF CURIOSITY
So cuuuute!

The same effect happens when you see a kitten or a puppy and find it so cute you just want to stroke and cuddle it! The "cuteness" is your instincts telling you that it's a baby that needs looking after.

Chapter 4

69

CHILDHOOD CHANGES

As children grow, they learn more and more new skills. In fact, you learn faster and can take in more information as a small child than at any other time in your life.

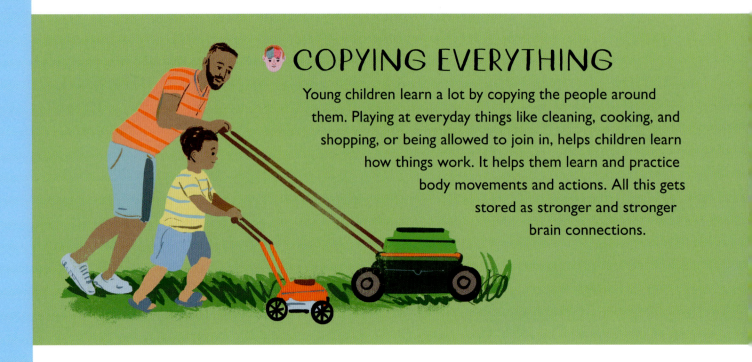

COPYING EVERYTHING

Young children learn a lot by copying the people around them. Playing at everyday things like cleaning, cooking, and shopping, or being allowed to join in, helps children learn how things work. It helps them learn and practice body movements and actions. All this gets stored as stronger and stronger brain connections.

LEARNING LANGUAGE

Children also learn to talk by copying, imitating the sounds they hear other people making. At an average of 12 months, they start saying some words. Over the next few years, they learn lots more words and how to form sentences. By the age of five, a typical child knows 10,000 words! At some stages, a child learns up to 20 new words every day.

As you get older, though, it becomes harder to learn new languages. The brain has a "window" of time during childhood when it is best at storing language words and grammar rules.

OUT OF CURIOSITY
Plastic brains

Psychologists sometimes describe brains as "plastic"—but it doesn't mean that they're made of plastic! Brain plasticity, or neuroplasticity, means the brain's ability to make new connections. It happens at all ages, but the brain is much more "plastic" when we're young.

This graph shows how brain plasticity for different skills peaks at different times.

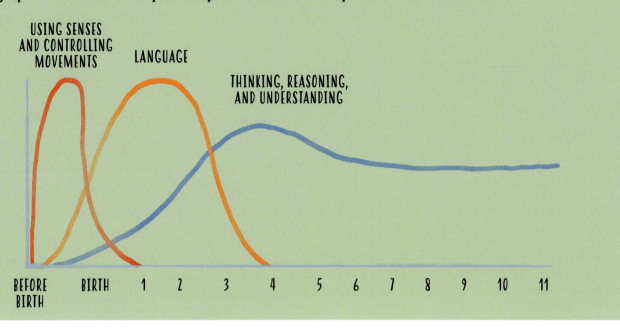

UNDERSTANDING AND LOGIC

It can take a little bit longer for children to learn to use their brains to figure things out. Psychologists have found that some abilities only develop as children get older.

For example, which of these two groups has more in it?

When you look at them and count them, you'll probably spot pretty soon that the second group has more. But a child under the age of five will probably choose the first group, because it looks bigger.

Chapter 4

71

TEENAGE BRAINS

From the age of about 10 or 11, children go through a series of changes known as puberty. This process takes several years and changes you from a child into an adult. Your body changes a lot, and so does your brain.

BRAIN PRUNING

Learning new things creates new brain connections. But the brain can also delete connections that aren't being used much. Brain scientists call this "synaptic pruning."

Synaptic pruning happens in young children, but the brain still makes more connections than it prunes. However, as puberty begins, the brain does a lot more pruning. The networks of neurons become simpler and clearer, but stronger and less "plastic." This process helps you grow up and think more clearly. But while it's happening, the brain may be less good at some things, making you feel confused or forgetful.

DURING CHILDHOOD, THE NUMBER OF CONNECTIONS IN THE BRAIN INCREASES.

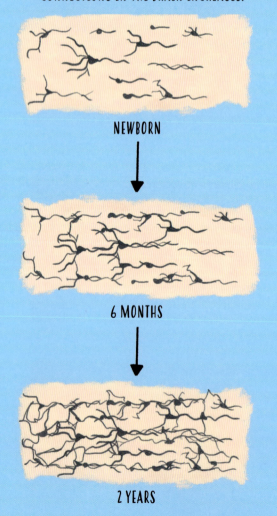

NEWBORN

6 MONTHS

2 YEARS

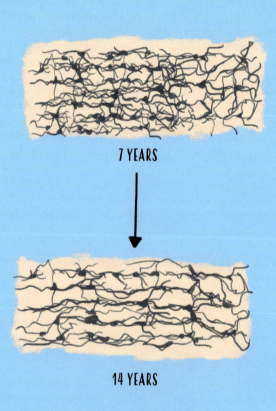

7 YEARS

14 YEARS

BUT BY 14 YEARS, PRUNING REDUCES THE NUMBER, MAKING CLEARER, STRONGER NETWORKS.

THOUGHTS AND EMOTIONS

Teenagers are often described as moody, impulsive, or more emotional—and this is partly because of changes in the brain.

In fact, the prefrontal cortex isn't fully mature until the age of about 25. So, during the teenage years, you're more likely to base actions on emotions and desires, and less on sensibly thinking things through.

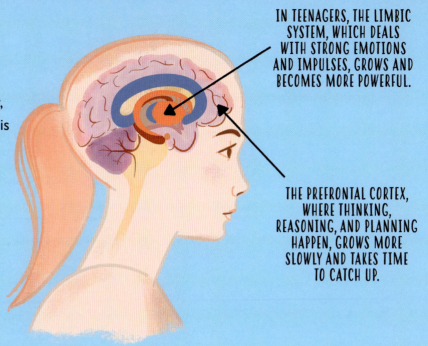

IN TEENAGERS, THE LIMBIC SYSTEM, WHICH DEALS WITH STRONG EMOTIONS AND IMPULSES, GROWS AND BECOMES MORE POWERFUL.

THE PREFRONTAL CORTEX, WHERE THINKING, REASONING, AND PLANNING HAPPEN, GROWS MORE SLOWLY AND TAKES TIME TO CATCH UP.

TEENAGE SELF-IMAGE

The teenage years are also a time when you move away from relying on your parents or carers for everything and become more independent. The teenage mind spends a lot of energy on building a self-image (see page 48) and a sense of identity, or who you are.

This may be why teenagers often …
- Care a lot more what their friends or classmates think than what their parents think.
- Rebel against parents or school rules.
- Experiment with different "identities," such as fashion styles and taste in music.
- Can easily feel self-conscious or embarrassed.

Chapter 4

73

THE ADULT BRAIN

All the growing up you do during puberty happens for a reason—so that you can live a grown-up life. People's brains keep changing during adulthood, too, and they often become more responsible and sensible as time goes on.

REDUCING RISK

Scientists have found that people under 25 are more likely than over-25's to do risky or dangerous things, such driving their car too fast and not wearing a seat belt. This is partly because of lack of experience. It's also because at around 25, the more thoughtful, rational frontal cortex takes over much more of your brain's decision-making.

OUT OF CURIOSITY
Impostor syndrome

Impostor syndrome is a feeling that you're not good enough to be doing what you're doing—like your job or being a parent. You feel like a fake, or "impostor," who will soon be "found out"! Amazingly, psychology studies have found that about 70% of people experience it, especially when they start a new job or responsibility.

NEW ROLES

When you become an adult, you'll probably have to get a job to earn a living. Many adults also become parents sometime in their 20s, 30s, or 40s. And instead of having parents to do it for you, you have to run a home, pay bills, and fix problems. These are all big changes that make demands on the brain and mind.

MORE ROLES AND RESPONSIBILITIES HELP THE BRAIN TO GET BETTER AT KEEPING TRACK OF THINGS, MAKING DECISIONS, AND MULTITASKING.

HOWEVER, THEY CAN ALSO CAUSE STRESS, WHICH CAN MAKE PEOPLE FEEL WORN OUT OR EVEN MAKE THEM ILL (SEE PAGE 100).

LIFE EXPERIENCES

Throughout life, we keep learning and changing. Life experience and events can change our brain connections, and they have an effect on our behavior or personality—in both helpful and not-so-helpful ways.

A BAD EXPERIENCE WITH A PARTICULAR FOOD CAN PUT YOU OFF IT FOR LIFE.

I'M NEVER EATING TOMATO SOUP AGAIN!

HAVING AN ACCIDENT FROM NOT WATCHING OUT FOR A RED LIGHT CAN MEAN BICYCLING MORE CARFULLY IN THE FUTURE.

OUCH!

OUCH!

Chapter 4

75

GETTING OLDER

You might have heard older people you know joking about becoming more forgetful, or being "set in their ways." Our brain power and mental abilities do change as we get older, but it's not just about losing abilities—we can get better at some things, too.

BRAIN CHANGES

As people get older, their bodies can start to wear out, work a little more slowly, or become less flexible—and it's the same for the brain. Physical changes in the brain include:

THE HIPPOCAMPUS, WHICH HELPS TO STORE MEMORIES, BECOMES WEAKER AND LESS EFFECTIVE.

BODY SYSTEMS THAT REPAIR AND PROTECT BRAIN CELLS STOP WORKING SO WELL (JUST AS THEY DO WITH THINGS LIKE SKIN AND EYE CELLS).

BLOOD FLOW REDUCES, WHICH MEANS BRAIN CELLS CAN GET A BIT LESS OXYGEN THAN THEY USED TO.

These changes can lead to effects such as:

SHORT-TERM MEMORY PROBLEMS, LIKE FORGETTING WHERE YOU PUT SOMETHING OR WHY YOU CAME INTO A ROOM.

SHOW ME HOW TO CHANGE THE SETTINGS AGAIN!

IT CAN GET HARDER TO LEARN NEW THINGS.

HOW CAN YOU DO THAT SO FAST?

AND THE BRAIN'S PROCESSING SPEED CAN SLOW DOWN.

MAXIMUM BRAIN POWER

However, some other brain skills can reach a peak in middle age. The brain and mind have learned from experience and have had lots of practice at solving problems, dealing with other people, and coming up with ideas. So middle-aged people are often good at leadership, managing complex situations, and making good decisions, even though they might not think as fast as they once did.

Think of country leaders, company bosses, or famous business leaders. They're often middle-aged, since that's when they have the knowledge and experience they need to take control.

Great artists, writers, and scientists often do their best work in middle age, after many years spent experimenting, learning, and improving their skills.

THE FAMOUS ARTIST, PICASSO, PAINTED HIS MOST RENOWNED WORK, GUERNICA, IN HIS 50S.

TOP CRIME WRITER AGATHA CHRISTIE WROTE HER MOST SUCCESSFUL BOOKS IN HER 40S AND 50S.

Chapter 4

77

OLDER AGE

When we get very old, body parts can stop working—and that can happen to the brain too. But it's different in different people, and there are things you can to help your brain stay healthy for longer.

THE AGING BRAIN

As you get older and older, your brain shrinks. From the age of 40, the brain loses about 5% of its volume every decade. Over 70, it shrinks even faster. Scientists aren't sure why, but it could be to do with the support cells around neurons that helps them carry electrical signals. If they start to die or become weaker, the neurons can't work as well. It gets harder to store new memories, learn new things, or make decisions.

YOUNG BRAIN   OLD BRAIN

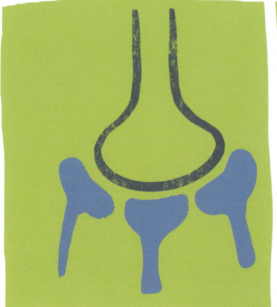
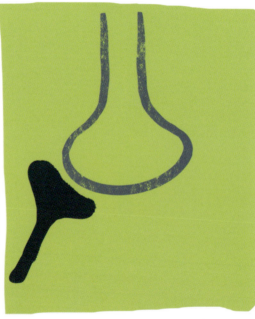

THE NUMBER OF CONNECTIONS BETWEEN NEURONS FALLS AS SOME NEURONS WORK LESS WELL.

AS THE VOLUME OF THE BRAIN SHRINKS, FLUID-FILLED GAPS CALLED VENTRICLES GET BIGGER, AND THE WRINKLES IN THE BRAIN GET DEEPER.

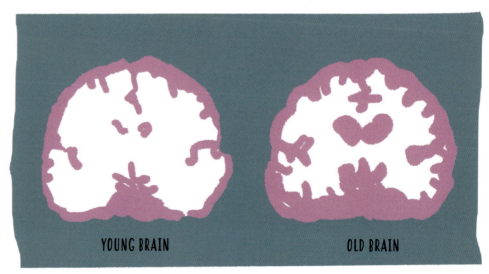

YOUNG BRAIN   OLD BRAIN

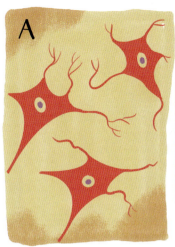

IN A HEALTHY BRAIN, THE NEURONS HAVE LOTS OF CONNECTIONS.

IN A BRAIN WITH ALZHEIMER'S DISEASE, PLAQUES AND TANGLES OF CHEMICALS DAMAGE AND BLOCK THE NEURONS.

DEMENTIA

Dementia is damage to the brain caused by some types of illnesses. It can happen to young people, but it's much more common in older age. One type happens when there's not enough blood flow to the brain. Another type, Alzheimer's disease, happens when chemicals collect in the brain, forming clusters called plaques, and damaging neurons.

USE IT OR LOSE IT

Dementia can cause problems like forgetfulness, confusion, getting words mixed up, and losing the ability to plan or organize things. But you can help your brain work better into old age, and reduce the risk of dementia, by keeping it active.

LIFELONG LEARNING

Learning and trying new things, such as sports, musical instruments, languages, or crafts, helps your brain's ability to form new connections and keep working.

BEING ACTIVE

Exercising your body helps, too. It releases chemicals that help neurons send signals, keeping them working for longer.

PUZZLES AND GAMES

Playing board games and video games, or doing puzzles and crosswords practices problem-solving and thinking skills, helping them to stay strong.

Chapter 4

79

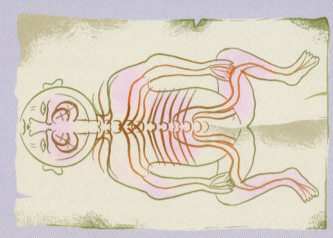

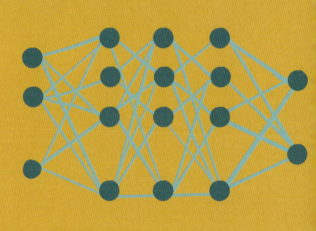

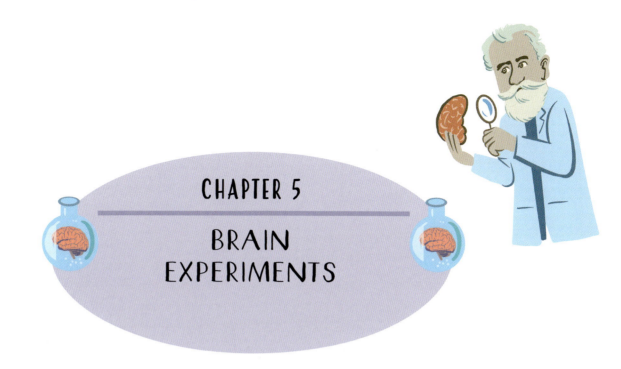

CHAPTER 5
BRAIN EXPERIMENTS

To find out as much as they can about how people's brains and minds work, psychologists and brain scientists do experiments. For example, they might try to find out how sleep affects our ability to learn or how illusions can fool the brain. Some scientists do experiments with babies and children to find out when different abilities develop or how babies learn. And some experiment with animals, testing things like animal intelligence.

To make sure experiments are accurate, scientists have to design them carefully, following a set of steps known as the scientific method. In this chapter, we'll find out how experiments work and explore some interesting brain and mind experiments.

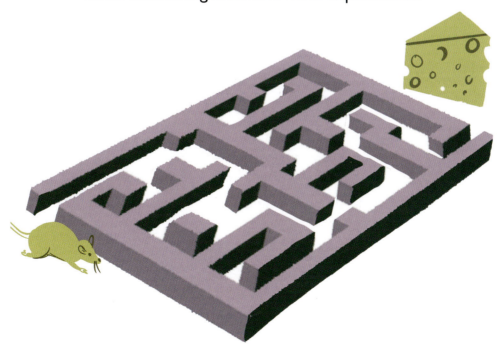

HOW IT STARTED

Since ancient times, people have tried to figure out what different body organs do. But long ago, the brain was a puzzle—people couldn't agree on what it was for!

ANCIENT BELIEFS

Three thousand years ago, when ancient Egyptians mummified people who had died, they threw away the brain, since they didn't think it was very important. They believed the heart, not the brain, contained a person's emotions and thoughts.

The ancient Chinese thought that the brain was a store of spare bone marrow (a soft substance inside bones). And ancient Greek scientist Aristotle believed that the brain's job was to let body heat escape.

EGYPTIAN MUMMY-MAKERS PRESERVED IMPORTANT ORGANS LIKE THE HEART IN SPECIAL JARS—BUT NOT THE BRAIN.

SCIENTIFIC STUDIES

However, not everyone agreed. Some ancient Greeks did believe that the brain was where thinking happened and dissected (cut open) animal brains to try to find out how they worked. Around 200 CE, famous Greek doctor Galen found that the brain was linked to the sense organs and sent signals to control the muscles.

GALEN LIVED IN THE TIME OF THE ROMAN EMPIRE, WHEN DISSECTING HUMAN BODIES WAS BANNED, SO HE STUDIED ANIMALS SUCH AS MONKEYS INSTEAD.

🐟 BRAIN, BODY, AND MIND

In the 1000s, Persian scientist and doctor Ibn Sina studied the brain and nervous system, and brain illnesses such as dementia and epilepsy. He invented medical treatments based on his experiments, and wrote about how each half of the brain controls half of the body.

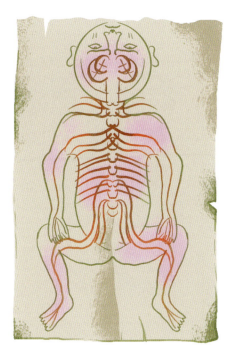

AN ILLUSTRATION OF THE BRAIN AND NERVOUS SYSTEM FROM ONE OF IBN SINA'S BOOKS

🐟 THE MODERN AGE

By the 1800s, more and more scientists were interested in brain science and psychology. They began to conduct more experiments on things like how the brain processes sense signals and which parts of the brain do what.

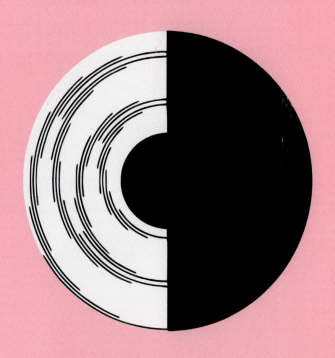

GERMAN SCIENTIST GUSTAV FECHNER EXPERIMENTED WITH THE SENSES AND VISUAL EFFECTS. IN THE 1830S, HE DISCOVERED THE FECHNER COLOR EFFECT, WHICH MAKES YOU SEE FAINT COLORS WHEN A BLACK AND WHITE DISK LIKE THIS IS SPINNING.

🐟 WUNDT'S LAB

In 1879, another German, Wilhelm Wundt, set up the first-ever psychology lab at Leipzig University in Germany to carry out psychology experiments.

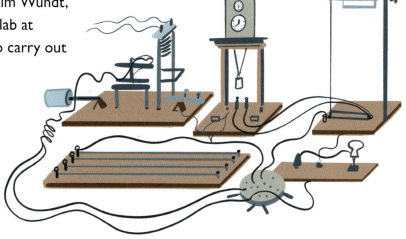

WUNDT USED EXPERIMENTAL EQUIPMENT LIKE THIS MACHINE FOR TESTING REACTION TIMES. IT MEASURED HOW FAST PEOPLE COULD PRESS A BUTTON AFTER SEEING A LIGHT FLASH OR HEARING A SOUND.

HOW EXPERIMENTS WORK

The scientific method is a way of doing experiments to make sure that your experiment will work properly, and you'll get useful results. Here's how it works …

1. OBSERVATION

Observation means watching situations to get ideas about what you want to find out.

2. ASK A QUESTION

Next, you come up with a question to find the answer to.

3. HYPOTHESIS

The hypothesis is the scientist's theory, or guess, at what the answer will be.

4. TESTING AND COLLECTING DATA

Next, you set up an experiment to measure the results in different situations. The things that can be different are known as variables. In this case, that's the amount of cheering and the performance.

FOR ONE GROUP, AN AUDIENCE WILL CLAP AND CHEER.

FOR ANOTHER, THEY'LL BOO AND SHOUT.

THE THIRD GROUP WILL HAVE NO AUDIENCE.

THEN THEY'LL ALL SWAP PLACES.

The test with no audience is called a "control."
It lets you compare your results to a normal situation.
When you carry out the experiment, you watch carefully and record the results.

	CHEERING AUDIENCE	BOOING AUDIENCE	NO AUDIENCE
TEAM 1	18 GOALS	15 GOALS	15 GOALS
TEAM 2	23 GOALS		
TEAM 3			

5. REPORT AND SHARE

Finally, you write a report, or "paper," about the results. Scientists publish their papers in magazines called journals, or talk about them at conferences, to share their work with each other.

WE FOUND THERE WERE MORE GOALS ON AVERAGE WHEN THE AUDIENCE CHEERED.
BUT WE ALSO NOTICED A SMALL NUMBER OF VOLUNTEERS DID BEST WITH NO AUDIENCE.
MAYBE IT'S BECAUSE THEY WERE INTROVERTED AND FELT EMBARRASSED?
THIS COULD BE AN IDEA FOR A NEW STUDY!

AVOIDING PROBLEMS

You have to try to make sure everything else in the test is as similar as possible. For example, you'd check that all your volunteers had a similar level of fitness and skill.

I'M A PROFESSIONAL SOCCER PLAYER!

SORRY, I CAN'T USE YOU FOR THIS EXPERIMENT!

And experiments must be ethical, meaning that you don't treat anyone badly or cause harm. For example, you wouldn't make volunteers play all day with no drinks or snacks!

Chapter 5

85

ANIMAL EXPERIMENTS

Animal psychology experiments can help us find out about their intelligence, how they communicate, and how to look after them. It sometimes helps us learn things about humans, too.

PAVLOV'S DOGS

Russian scientist Ivan Pavlov carried out this famous experiment in the 1890s. He was studying digestion in dogs. The dogs drooled when they were fed (since saliva helps animals swallow their food). Pavlov noticed that they also drooled when they saw an assistant coming, since they were expecting to be fed.

1. PAVLOV NOTICED THAT DOGS DROOLED AND DRIBBLED WHEN IT WAS FEEDING TIME.

2. PAVLOV SET UP AN EXPERIMENT WHERE HE MADE A NOISE JUST BEFORE THE DOGS WERE FED.

3. THE DOGS STARTED DROOLING AS SOON AS THEY HEARD THE SOUND.

4. THEY EVEN DROOLED IF THERE WAS JUST THE SOUND AND NO FOOD.

CONDITIONING

This is known in psychology as conditioning, and it happens in humans, too. It's part of an area of psychology called behaviorism, based on the idea that we learn ways of reacting and behaving from our experiences.

For example, Rosie loves seeing her grandma.

GRANDMA WEARS LAVENDER PERFUME.

WHENEVER ROSIE SMELLS LAVENDER, SHE FEELS HAPPY.

ANIMAL BRAINS

Animas can't do a human IQ test (see page 41), but scientists can test their intelligence in other ways.

In this test, an octopus was given a screw-top jar with a treat inside. The octopus figured out how to twist it around to open it.

Mazes can be used to study how animals like rats learn. The more times they are put in the maze, the faster they run through it, since they are learning the route and mapping it in their heads. This has helped psychologists to understand human learning, too.

NINE BRAINS

Octopuses are very intelligent and very interesting for brain scientists. They have one main brain and eight mini brains, one for each arm!

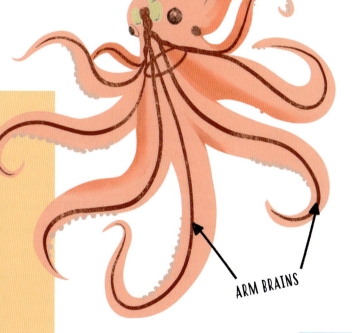

MAKING ANIMALS HAPPIER

Some scientists study animas in zoos and on farms to measure how stressed or bored they are, and to find out what helps them stay calm and happy.

ZOOS GIVE ANIMALS TOYS THAT HELP THEM RECREATE THEIR NATURAL BEHAVIOR, LIKE HUNTING AND EXPLORING, TO REDUCE STRESS.

BABIES AND CHILDREN

Experiments with babies look at what they pay attention to and how they pick up information from around them.

OOH – THAT'S INTERESTING!

UNDERSTANDING BABIES

How do you get babies to take part in experiments? Brain scientists have some clever ways of understanding what's going on in baby brains.

For example, they've found that babies usually look at something for longer if it's surprising or new—probably because their brains are always trying to take in new information. They will also suck for longer on a pacifier or dummy when experiencing something new.

I'VE HEARD THAT BEFORE!

One experiment found that babies learn the sound of their mother's language while in the womb from hearing her speak.

Soon after birth, babies were played sounds from their mother's language and sounds from a different language. They were more surprised and interested in the foreign language, showing they could tell the difference.

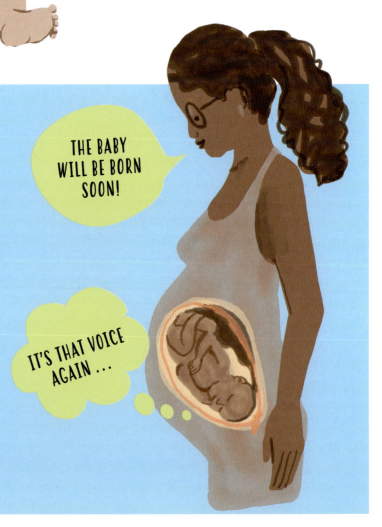

THE BABY WILL BE BORN SOON!

IT'S THAT VOICE AGAIN …

STAGES OF UNDERSTANDING

Psychologists also do experiments to study cognitive development. Children go through several stages of understanding as they begin to use reason, logic, and imagination, and psychologists have come up with some clever tests to show this.

One famous experiment is known as the Sally-Anne test (though there are many different versions of it). Children are shown two dolls acting out a story.

SALLY HAS A BASKET, AND ANNE HAS A BOX.

SALLY PUTS HER BALL IN HER BASKET, THEN GOES OUT FOR A WALK.

ANNE TAKES THE BALL OUT OF THE BASKET AND HIDES IT IN HER BOX.

SALLY COMES BACK. WHERE WILL SHE LOOK FOR HER BALL?

You'd probably say that Sally will look in her basket, where she left it. But children under the age of about four or five usually get this wrong.

THEORY OF MIND

Why? Because *they* know the ball is in the box, and they haven't yet developed the ability to understand that Sally has a different point of view. It takes children time to learn to see things from someone else's point of view—an ability psychologists call "theory of mind."

Chapter 5

89

PERCEPTION EXPERIMENTS

Perception means how we perceive, or experience, what's happening around us through our senses. Experiments show how the brain plays a huge part in what we think is going on, by changing, filtering, and mixing up information.

🦍 THE McGURK EFFECT

For this experiment, scientists show people a movie of someone saying a sound. It shows the speaker making a "B" sound with their lips and saying "Ba."

Then they show the person using their teeth and lips to make an "F" sound. The sound being played is still "Ba," but people watching the movie think it's "Fa."

B   F

This shows how our brains combine information from different senses. If it doesn't match up, your brain tries to make a guess—usually trusting sight more than sound.

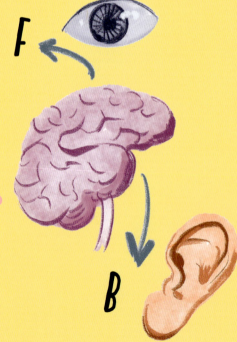

Chapter 5

90

🦍 THE HIDDEN GORILLA

We also filter out information we don't need, so that we can focus our attention on what's important. In one experiment, scientists showed people a video of two teams throwing balls to each other. They had to try and count how many times one of the teams passed the ball. This was difficult, so they had to really concentrate.

Afterward, the viewers were asked if they'd spotted someone in a gorilla suit walking through the game. Around half of them hadn't! Our brains are so good at blocking out other things to let us focus, they could even ignore the gorilla.

🦍 WHAT DO THINGS LOOK LIKE?

You probably think you know what most things look like. After all, you can recognize them when you see them. But British psychologist Anne Treisman believed that we actually piece together separate details to "build" an object in our minds—a theory known as "feature integration."

To test this, try drawing a bicycle (without looking at one). Most people find that, although they can easily recognize a bicycle, it's hard to remember how it looks as a whole.

PEOPLE KNOW A BIKE HAS WHEELS, A FRAME, A SEAT, AND HANDLEBARS—BUT NOT EXACTLY HOW THEY FIT TOGETHER!

THIS IS WHAT A BIKE REALLY LOOKS LIKE!

Chapter 5

91

THE INFLUENCE OF OTHERS

What would you do if you *knew* something was true, but everyone around you disagreed? A psychologist named Solomon Asch designed an amazing experiment to test this.

HOW LONG IS THE STICK?

Asch took a group of eight students and showed them all a card with a line on it and another card with three lines marked A, B, and C.

Then he asked them to say which of the three matched the first line. However, only one person in the experiment—the last one to be asked—was really being tested. They didn't know that the others were all actors! Asch tested several volunteers in this way.

WHAT HAPPENED?

If the actors all chose C, so did the last person. But sometimes, the actors were told beforehand to all choose A, or all choose B.

When this happened, quite a few of the people being tested—around a third of them—said the same as everyone else, even though they could clearly see that C was right.

CONFORMERS AND REBELS

Psychologists still do similar experiments, testing which groups or types of people are most likely to conform, or go along with everyone else. Afterward, when they find out the truth, people often say they *did* think they knew the right answer, but ignored it to fit in!

Whether people do this partly depends on personality (see page 38). One of the "Big Five" personality traits, agreeableness, is about how much you want to fit in or care what others think of you. What do you think you would have chosen?

OUT OF CURIOSITY
The influence of scientists

When people know that they're doing an experiment with scientists watching them, that could change their reactions and affect the results. Scientists try to avoid this in various ways.

In one experiment, scientists wanted to find out if people would help someone who was injured. They set up two different, fake experiments in two buildings and asked the people taking part to walk from one to the other for the second test.

On the way, an actor pretended to be an injured person on the ground. This was the actual experiment—but the people being tested didn't know that! They thought it was real life, so they behaved like they would normally.

Chapter 5

93

MEMORY TESTS

Memory is a very important part of our brains and minds. Experiments help scientists find out how it works, and how to make learning easier or more effective.

THE EXPERIMENTS OF EBBINGHAUS

German scientist Hermann Ebbinghaus studied memory in the 1880s, in the early days of psychology experiments. He used strings of made-up nonsense words, measuring how long it took to memorize them and forget them again, and which methods worked best.

Today, we know that experimenting on yourself can lead to "bias," meaning that you might influence your own results, even if you don't mean to. However, Ebbinghaus still discovered a lot of interesting things that are still used in psychology today.

LEARNING CURVE

You learn fastest on your first attempt to learn something. On later attempts, you'll learn more and more slowly. This is now known as the "learning curve."

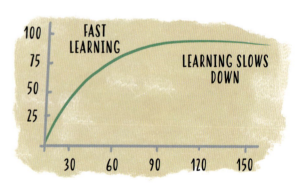

FIRST AND LAST

The first and last items in a string of information are the easiest to memorize.

SPACE IT OUT

You learn better if you space out your learning sessions, with breaks in between.

IT'S IN THERE SOMEWHERE!

Even if you think you've totally forgotten something, it's easier to learn it a second time. This shows that memories get stored in our unconscious minds (see page 28).

Chapter 5

94

DIGIT SPANS

Scientists often use "digit span" as a measurement of memory. It means how many digits (numbers or letters) you can remember in the right order. To test it, they give people longer and longer strings of digits to remember, until they stop being able to do it. They've found that most adults have a digit span of between 5 and 9.

4
74
532
7123
87678 ← MOST PEOPLE FIND IT PRETTY EASY UP TO 5 DIGITS.
359812
3615823
68267384 ← AT AROUND 8, IT STARTS GETTING REALLY HARD...
756387465

87678   359812   3615...???

UUGH, I'M STUCK!

CHUNKING

Other experiments show that people find it much easier to remember digit strings if they can break them down into groups, a method called "chunking."

For example, try learning these three strings of six numbers. Which is easiest?

267854
333462
595959

Most people find the second and third ones easiest, since they can organize them into chunks or patterns. Psychologists think that this helps because it uses up less brain power.

Chapter 5

95

COMPUTER MODELS

Computer modeling, or computer simulation, uses computerized versions of real-life situations to do experiments and test theories. It's very useful in all kinds of science, especially psychology and brain science.

💻 HOW DOES IT WORK?

You've probably played computer games that imitate, or "simulate," something from real life—like a car race or a building game.

A scientific computer model is similar, but instead of playing it like a game, scientists use it to test what happens in different situations. For example, a flood simulation could use map and weather information to show which areas will get flooded in heavy rain.

HMM, LOOKS LIKE THERE'S A MAJOR FLOOD RISK IN SOUTH RIVERTOWN!

MODELING BEHAVIOR

Some psychologists study how people behave in big crowds.
This is important for safety, for example, at festivals or sports stadiums, to make sure people don't get crushed together. But it's hard to get thousands of volunteers to experiment with and could be dangerous.

So they often use computer simulations instead. They contain individual "people," each programmed to behave like a real person and to react to other people in the simulation.

You can set the simulation to model crowds moving around in different situation—such as testing stadium or museum designs to see which are safest.

A SIMULATION OF AN EMERGENCY EVACUATION, WITH EVERYONE MOVING THROUGH THE EXITS

INDIVIDUALS IN THE SIMULATION

OUT OF CURIOSITY
Simulated worm

We can't make a model of a whole human brain, since it's so complicated. But scientists have made a computer model of the brain and nervous system of a tiny worm.

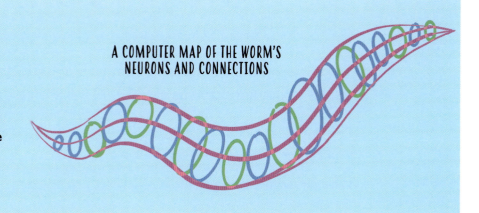

A COMPUTER MAP OF THE WORM'S NEURONS AND CONNECTIONS

COMPUTER BRAINS

In our brains, neurons are linked together in networks, so that signals can travel between them (see page 13). We can make computer models of these networks that work in the same way. They're called neural networks, and they're used to study how the brain works and to create artificial intelligence, or AI.

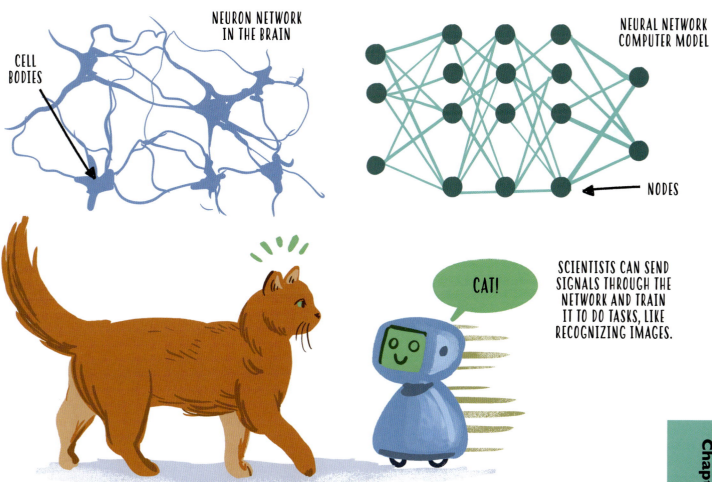

NEURON NETWORK IN THE BRAIN

CELL BODIES

NEURAL NETWORK COMPUTER MODEL

NODES

CAT!

SCIENTISTS CAN SEND SIGNALS THROUGH THE NETWORK AND TRAIN IT TO DO TASKS, LIKE RECOGNIZING IMAGES.

SOME ROBOTS CAN "SEE" USING CAMERAS COMBINED WITH NEURAL NETWORKS THAT CAN IDENTIFY OBJECTS.

Chapter 5

AMAZING EFFECTS

Some brain science experiments have unexpected, strange, or mind-boggling results that seem hard to explain. Here are just a few fascinating examples …

THE STROOP TEST

In this experiment, named after American psychologist J. Ridley Stroop, you look at a grid of color names, like this. You have to say what color you can see—not what the word says.

When the words match their colors, it's easy. But when they don't, your brain gets very confused! Most people find it takes much longer to say the right colors in test 2. The part of your brain that sees colors has to fight with the part that reads the words, and this slows you down or makes you get stuck.

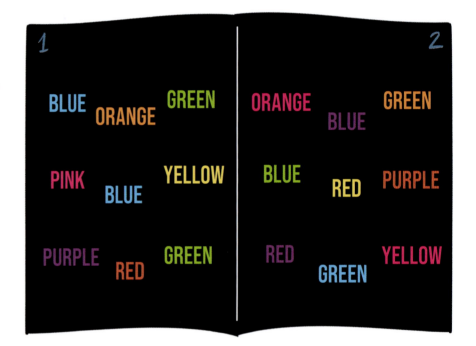

MIRROR MIX-UP

Can you draw a shape while looking in a mirror? It doesn't sound too hard, but try it!

Sit or stand in front of a mirror with a pad of paper and a pen. Look at them only in the mirror. You could use some card to block your view of the real paper and pen, like this.

It's VERY hard! Your brain is used to making your hands move using information from your eyes. In the mirror, what your eyes see is flipped, leaving your brain confused.

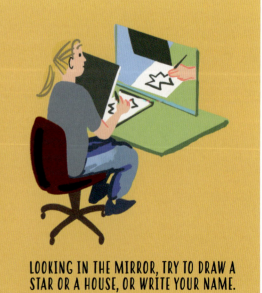

LOOKING IN THE MIRROR, TRY TO DRAW A STAR OR A HOUSE, OR WRITE YOUR NAME.

UPSIDE-DOWN WORLD

What would happen if you wore goggles that made everything look totally upside down? Psychologists have actually tried this. At first, people wearing the goggles were very confused and struggled with everyday activities. But after about ten days, their brains adapted, and things looked normal to them!

THE PLACEBO EFFECT

Imagine that you went to the doctor with a twisted ankle, and they gave you some fake pills to make it feel better.

Well, they might actually work, thanks to the placebo effect! Experiments show that fake medical treatments, or placebos, often *do* help. Your brain somehow thinks you are being treated, and you feel better. Even more amazingly, it still works even if you know it's fake!

Chapter 5

99

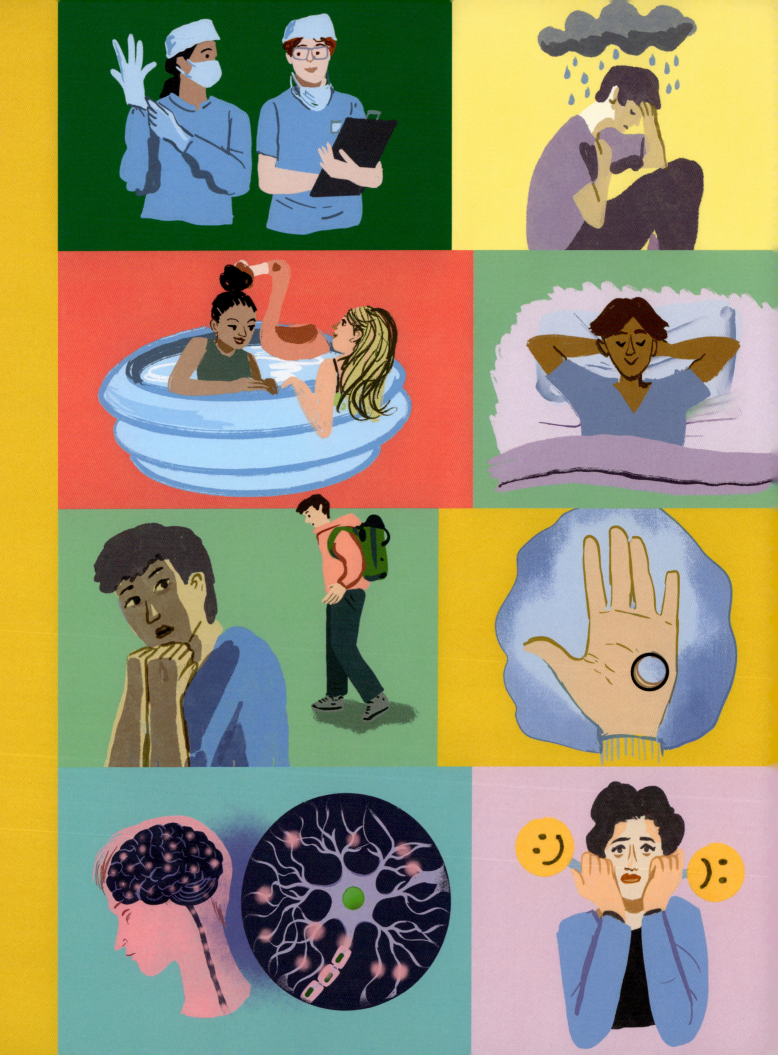

CHAPTER 6

MENTAL HEALTH AND ILLNESS

Many psychologists and brain experts spend their time doing experiments and writing about their discoveries. But some have a different job—they work in health care, helping people who have mental illnesses or problems with their brains.

Just as the human body can have health problems, so can the mind. Mental means "of the mind," and a mental illness is a problem with mental processes, such as thoughts, emotions, or perceptions. There are many types of mental illnesses, but there are also lots of treatments for them. The brain can be affected by illnesses and injuries that affect the mind, too. Sometimes, they even help to reveal how the brain works.

In this chapter, we'll find out about illnesses of the mind and brain, what causes them and how they can be treated, and how everyone can help themselves to stay mentally healthy.

FEELING STRESSED!

One of the most common mental problems, which most people experience sometimes, is stress. Stress isn't always bad—it's a natural response to danger or pressure, and it can help us to survive. But too much stress can be harmful.

🤯 WHAT IS STRESS?

Stress is a state of tension, fear, worry, or alertness caused by the situation you're in. It evolved to help us deal with difficult or scary situations.

Imagine that a volcano erupts just as you're walking past.

Your brain realizes you're in danger and triggers your body to release hormones (body chemicals) to help you to react.

DANGER INCOMING!

PREPARE FOR ACTION!

OH NO! YIKES!

BOOOM!

PHEW! THAT WAS CLOSE!

RUN FOR IT!

For example, adrenaline is a stress hormone. It makes your heart beat faster, so that it pumps more blood to your muscles and you can move quickly.

🙍 WHEN STRESS IS A PROBLEM

Stress hormones can be very useful, but if we have too much of them, especially for a long time, it's not very good for our brains and bodies. If you're always feeling stressed and worried, it can make you unwell—both in your body and in your mind.

EFFECTS ON THE BODY

HEADACHES
POUNDING HEART
TIGHT, SORE MUSCLES
STOMACHACHES
TROUBLE SLEEPING, MAKING YOU FEEL EXHAUSTED
WEAKENS YOUR IMMUNE SYSTEM, THE BODY SYSTEM THAT FIGHTS GERMS—SO YOU CATCH COLDS AND OTHER BUGS MORE EASILY.

EFFECTS ON THE MIND

FEELING SAD AND WEEPY
FEELING GRUMPY OR EASILY IRRITATED
TROUBLE CONCENTRATING
FORGETFULNESS
LOSING YOUR APPETITE
CAN LEAD TO MORE SERIOUS MENTAL ILLNESSES, SUCH AS DEPRESSION (SEE PAGE 104).

🙍 MODERN STRESS

Any difficult or scary situation can cause stress—like being bullied, being chased by a dog, or being involved in an accident, a natural disaster, or even a war. But some experts think the modern world causes stress in other ways, too.

- Pressure from doing a job, being responsible for a home and family, and paying bills.
- Worrying about school, homework, or exams.
- Social media, smartphones, and 24-hour news that make it hard to escape from constant messages and scary news stories.

Chapter 6

103

🌧️ TYPES OF MENTAL ILLNESSES 🌧️

As with physical diseases in the body, there are lots of different kinds of mental illness. They can be different in different people, and it's possible to have two or more mental illnesses at the same time. Here are some of them.

I JUST CAN'T FACE DOING ANYTHING...

DEPRESSION

People sometimes use the word *depressed* to describe normal sadness, but real depression is more severe and long-lasting. It can make you feel numb, hopeless, worthless, and lacking any energy to do things.

BIPOLAR DISORDER

Bipolar means "two poles," or two extremes. People who have it can alternate between feeling depressed and a high-energy, overexcited state known as mania.

SO MANY THINGS COULD GO WRONG!

ANXIETY OR PANIC DISORDER

Everyone feels anxious sometimes, but if you have an anxiety disorder, you can't stop worrying. It can also cause panic attacks, where your body tenses up or you feel like you can't breathe.

PTSD

PTSD is short for Post-Traumatic Stress Disorder, which people can have after a dangerous or frightening experience. They might feel easily annoyed or startled, be unable to sleep, or have nightmares and "flashbacks," where their mind replays what they went through.

OCD

Short for Obsessive-Compulsive Disorder, OCD has many different forms. It can give you constant worrying thoughts, make you want to check things over and over, or go through endless rituals that make you feel safe. It can use up lots of time and energy, leaving you exhausted.

PHOBIAS

A phobia is an extreme fear of something that's out of proportion to how dangerous it actually is. People can have phobias of all sorts of things—like insects, bridges, wide-open spaces, cats, vomiting, or going to the dentist.

EATING DISORDERS

An eating disorder affects the way people feel about food. They might feel scared of eating and avoid it, or compulsively eat too much, making themselves sick.

SCHIZOPHRENIA

This severe mental illness can make people believe things that aren't true. They might feel that someone is giving them secret instructions or that they can do impossible things. They can become detached from real life and unable to look after themselves.

Chapter 6

105

WHAT CAUSES MENTAL ILLNESS?

Psychologists have discovered a lot about mental illnesses, but they don't still fully understand how they work. They often seem to have several different causes that work together to make someone become unwell.

GENES AND DNA

Several types of mental illness run in families, including OCD, anxiety, and schizophrenia. Some people have genes, passed on in DNA from parents to their children, that make them more likely to get a mental illness. But having the genes doesn't mean they definitely will.

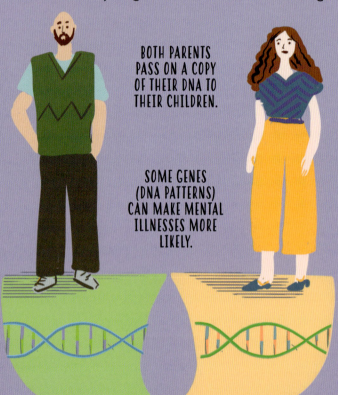

BOTH PARENTS PASS ON A COPY OF THEIR DNA TO THEIR CHILDREN.

SOME GENES (DNA PATTERNS) CAN MAKE MENTAL ILLNESSES MORE LIKELY.

There's also another way it could work—how parents bring up their children and what their family life is like.

For example, if a child's parents are very anxious and worry about danger a lot, the child could pick up on that and become anxious, too.

🙁 STRESSFUL SITUATIONS

Another big cause of mental illness is stressful, upsetting, harmful, or dangerous experiences. That includes a wide range of possible things, such as …

- Being in a war, disaster, or accident
- Being attacked, hurt, or injured
- Being bullied or discriminated against
- Having a physical illness or disability that makes life difficult
- Being overworked or having too much to do
- Losing someone you love, or having to leave your home
- Feeling lonely, powerless, or trapped in a situation

Having bad experiences as a child often has an effect—especially being neglected and not looked after properly, or not given enough love and affection as a baby (see page 68).

However, a bad experience on its own doesn't always cause mental illness. Instead, scientists think it could trigger illness in someone who has particular genes, a particular personality type, or other risk factors.

🙁 LIFESTYLE AND SURROUNDINGS

What's around you and the way you live can be important, too. Things like an unhealthy diet, a cold or moldy home, and living in poverty make physical illnesses more likely, and they seem to increase the risk of mental illness, too. So do smoking, using drugs and alcohol, and some kinds of pollution in the air or in drinking water.

Chapter 6

107

TREATMENTS AND THERAPIES

A clinical psychologist is an expert on the mind, who is trained to help people with mental illnesses. It usually involves helping the person to talk and think about their feelings.

 ## TALKING IT OVER

How can talking about an illness help to make it better? Mental illnesses can affect the way you think, making you confused. If someone has had a bad experience, they might try to suppress, or squash down, bad feelings and try to ignore them. But this can make things worse, because the brain needs to "process" experiences and make sense of them.

I'M SO SCARED OF DOGS, I SOMETIMES CAN'T LEAVE THE HOUSE.

WHAT IS IT ABOUT THEM THAT SCARES YOU?

In talking therapy, a psychologist asks questions and listens to the patient talk about their experiences and emotions. They don't judge or jump to conclusions, but help the patient think about and understand their feelings. Usually, the patient has regular sessions for a few weeks or months, gradually figuring out more about what's happening.

CAN YOU REMEMBER WHEN YOU FIRST FELT LIKE THIS?

WHEN I WAS FIVE, AND MY PARENTS SPLIT UP. MY MOTHER'S NEW BOYFRIEND HAD A BIG DOG, AND I DIDN'T LIKE IT. I THINK MY FEELINGS FROM THAT TIME ARE MIXED UP WITH DOGS.

GET MOVING!

Psychologists have found that exercise is one of the most effective treatments of all for mental illnesses, especially depression, anxiety, and stress. But why?

- It releases brain chemicals called endorphins that reduce pain and make you feel good.

- It can distract you from stressful situations.

- Being outdoors in fresh air and natural surroundings helps people feel calmer (maybe because we evolved to live in nature).

- It tires you out, helping you to sleep better.

- If you exercise in a group or play a sport, you see friends, which can cheer you up.

- And it can feel good to achieve something, like scoring a goal or climbing a mountain.

TRAINING THE BRAIN

Some psychologists use therapy methods that help your brain to learn to recognize difficult thoughts and feelings, and change how you react to them. One is CBT, short for Cognitive Behavioral Therapy. It's useful for anxiety, OCD, PTSD, and phobias.

The patient learns to recognize their patterns of thoughts, feelings, and behavior …

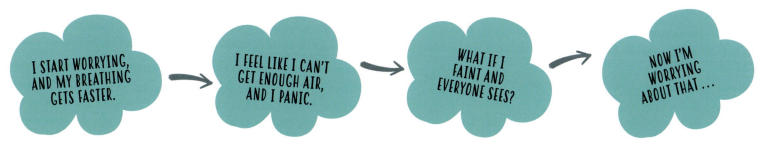

… and change or redirect them:

Chapter 6

109

MIND MEDICINE

We take medicines for physical illnesses, like asthma or headaches, and there are some medicines that can treat mental illnesses too.

BRAIN CHEMICALS

The brain contains chemicals called neurotransmitters, which help signals jump from one neuron to the next. Different kinds of chemicals have different effects, especially on emotions. For example:

- Endorphins reduce pain and make you feel happy and well.
- Serotonin helps control your moods.
- Dopamine pays a part in pleasure and motivation, the drive to do things.

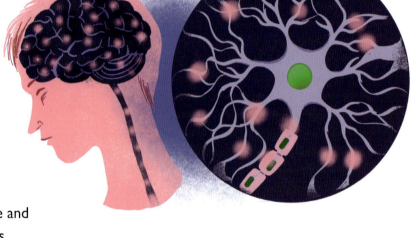

In some mental illnesses, such as bipolar disorder and schizophrenia, the person has an imbalance of neurotransmitters in their brain. They can take medicines that work by blocking or increasing the flow of different neurotransmitters to get the balance right.

OUT OF CURIOSITY
A hole in the head!

Skulls dating from hundreds or thousands of years go have been found with holes drilled or carved into them. This is called trepanning, and many ancient peoples used it as a treatment for mental health problems, as well as headaches and other diseases. Experts think they may have done it to try to release evil spirits that they believed were causing the illnesses.

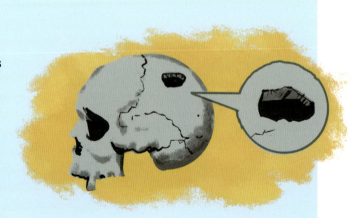

HELPING YOU RELAX

Stress, anxiety, and panic can make your muscles tense up and your heart beat faster, making it impossible to relax and calm down, and making it hard to sleep. Tight muscles in your back and neck can cause pain, too.

So some people take medicines to deal with these problems.
- Medicines called beta blockers can slow down a speeding heartbeat.
- Muscle relaxant medicines stop muscles from being so tense.
- Sleeping pills contain medicines that slow down your brain processes, helping you to feel tired.

These medicines can't treat the causes of mental illnesses and might not make them go away, but they can help patients manage the symptoms.

EATING RIGHT

Some types of food are very good for the brain and help it to work better, so they can help people who have a mental illness, too.

Healthy fats help the brain to keep working well. They're found in olive oil, avocados, nuts, seeds, and oily fish like salmon and mackerel.

Vitamins, especially B vitamins, can help to improve your mood. Fresh fruit and vegetables, eggs, meat, dairy products and breakfast cereals are all sources of vitamins.

Bananas, dark chocolate, chicken, tomatoes, berries, and yoghurt all contain chemicals that help your brain, too.

Chapter 6

111

BRAIN DAMAGE

Since the brain is important and very delicate, it's protected by a hard, thick skull and several layers of tough coverings.

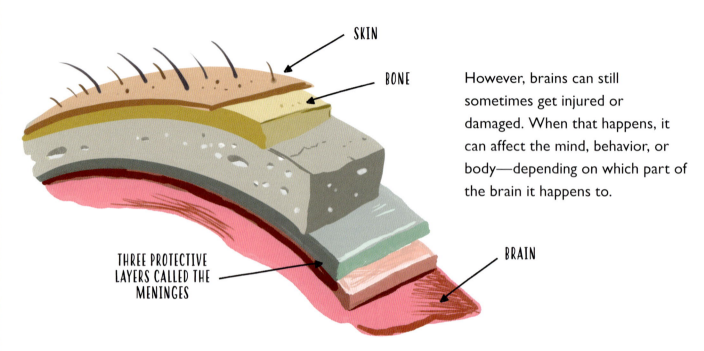

- SKIN
- BONE
- THREE PROTECTIVE LAYERS CALLED THE MENINGES
- BRAIN

However, brains can still sometimes get injured or damaged. When that happens, it can affect the mind, behavior, or body—depending on which part of the brain it happens to.

THE STRANGE CASE OF PHINEAS GAGE

In 1848, a worker named Phineas Gage was pushing explosives into a hole in a rock to blast out a path for a railroad, using a metal tool called a tamping iron. But he accidentally scraped the rock, making a spark. A sudden explosion blew the iron out of the hole—and right through Gage's skull.

Amazingly, he survived—but his doctors reported that his personality changed. He had been a responsible, sensible team leader. After the accident, he became rude, impatient, stubborn, and moody, and found it hard to control his emotions.

THIS PICTURE SHOWS WHERE THE TAMPING IRON WENT THROUGH GAGE'S HEAD.

Chapter 6

112

CLUES FROM THE BRAIN

Gage damaged his frontal lobe—the brain area that does reasoning and decision-making, and helps to control emotions and instincts—which explains why his personality changed. Brain injuries like this have helped brain scientists understand what different parts of the brain do.

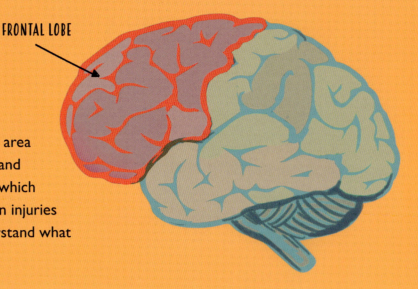
FRONTAL LOBE

DAMAGED AREA

DAMAGED AREA

BLOOD CLOT

LEAKING BLOOD VESSEL

STROKES

A stroke happens when a blood vessel in the brain gets blocked or breaks, cutting off blood flow to a particular area.

Like brain injuries, strokes also help to reveal how the brain works. Depending on which brain area is damaged, they affect the patient in different ways—such as ...

- Being weak or paralyzed on the opposite side of the body to where the stroke is.
- Being unable to talk and hold a conversation—but still able to remember and sing songs, since they're stored in a separate part of the brain.
- Being unable to see or understand one side of what's in front of you.
- Losing the ability to recognize objects.

Scientists sometimes test stroke patients to find out how it's affected them, for example, by asking them to draw a clock. A drawing like this shows that the patient can't process or understand one side of their field of vision.

Chapter 6

BRAIN SURGERY

Sometimes doctors can fix brain damage or diseases with brain surgery. As you can imagine, it's very complex and difficult to do. Brain surgeons, also called neurosurgeons, have to train for around 15 years to learn to do it.

TYPES OF BRAIN SURGERY

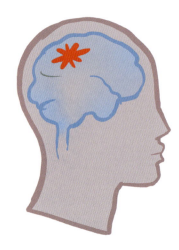

STROKES
When a stroke (see page 113) is damaging the brain, a surgeon can seal off a broken blood vessel or remove a blood clot.

EPILEPSY
Epilepsy is a brain disease that affects the electrical signals in the brain. It can cause seizures that make patient collapse, shake, or become unconscious, and they can be dangerous. Sometimes, surgeons can treat epilepsy by removing a small part of the brain, or by implanting a device that regulates the electrical signals.

OUT OF CURIOSITY
Staying awake

Sometimes, patients are kept awake during surgery, so that the surgeon can make sure they don't damage anything! The patient still has painkilling medicine, but they can answer questions to make sure important brain parts are still working.

BRAIN TUMORS
A brain tumor is a lump or mass that grows in the brain. Sometimes it's a kind of cancer, which can spread to other areas. Other brain tumors are not cancer, but they can cause problems by pressing on and squashing the rest of the brain. Depending on where it is, a surgeon may be able to excise the tumor, or cut it out.

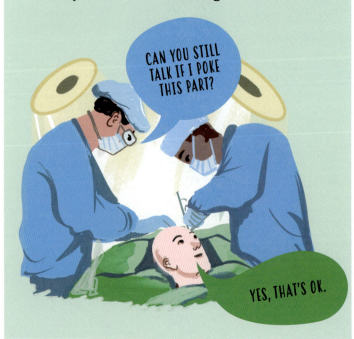

WHAT HAPPENS?

Before surgery, the patient is usually given a general anesthesia—medicine that sends them to sleep and makes sure they can't feel any pain.

Sometimes, the surgeon removes a section of skull and cuts through the meninges (see page 112) to access the brain. For other operations, they can reach the right place by drilling a small hole or entering through a blood vessel from another part of the body.

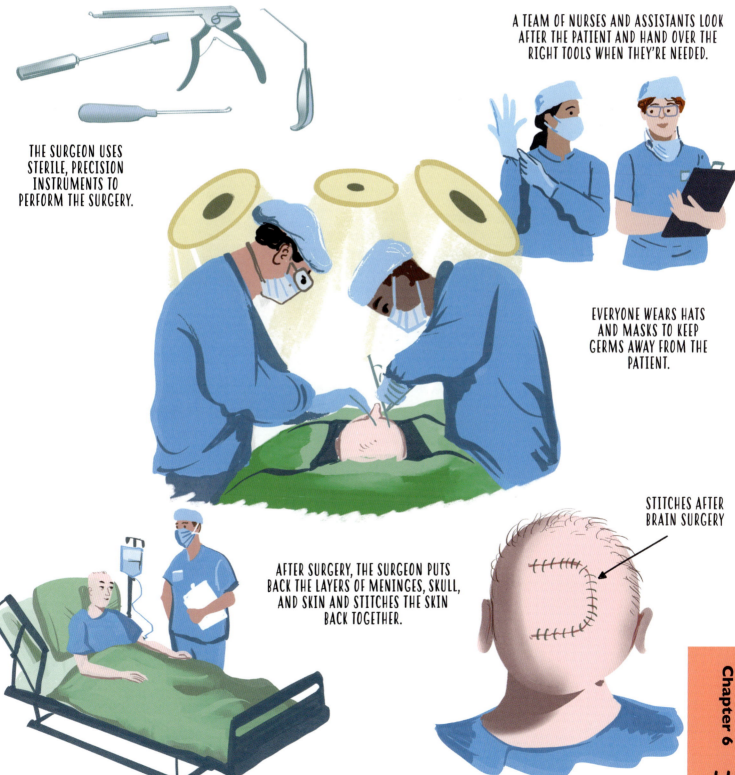

THE SURGEON USES STERILE, PRECISION INSTRUMENTS TO PERFORM THE SURGERY.

A TEAM OF NURSES AND ASSISTANTS LOOK AFTER THE PATIENT AND HAND OVER THE RIGHT TOOLS WHEN THEY'RE NEEDED.

EVERYONE WEARS HATS AND MASKS TO KEEP GERMS AWAY FROM THE PATIENT.

AFTER SURGERY, THE SURGEON PUTS BACK THE LAYERS OF MENINGES, SKULL, AND SKIN AND STITCHES THE SKIN BACK TOGETHER.

STITCHES AFTER BRAIN SURGERY

Chapter 6

115

STAYING HEALTHY

How can you keep your mind, and your brain, as healthy as possible? There are lots of ways to look after them, and they're easy to fit into everyday life.

GET EXERCISE

Sports, swimming, fitness classes, or just walking or bicycling around are all good for your mental health.

DE-STRESS!

You can't always avoid stress, but you can counteract it or reduce it by doing de-stressing activities. Find the things that work best for you, then try to do some of them every day.

Cuddling a pet

Going outdoors

A warm bath or shower

Listening to or playing music

Looking at something that makes you laugh, like a funny book or TV show, or joking with friends

Talking about your feelings

Doing something creative or artistic

Helping someone with something

Playing a sport

Dancing

INTERACT

Talking and doing things with others helps you feel connected and cared about. It could be family members, friends, people you do a club or activity with, and even pets.

SLEEP WELL!

Sleep helps your brain and mind to work well, learn and remember things, and feel relaxed, so it's important to get enough.

GET OUTDOORS

Spend time in nature if you can, even if it's just a local park or garden. It helps our minds to feel calm.

PROTECT YOUR BRAIN

You can also take steps to keep your brain healthy and protect it from damage.

Always wear a helmet for riding a bike, skateboarding, or any other activity where you could fall and hit your head.

Recreational drugs can harm your brain. Even when you're an adult, avoid smoking or vaping, too much alcohol, and illegal drugs such as cannabis.

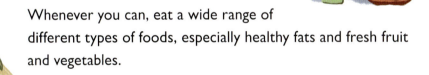

Whenever you can, eat a wide range of different types of foods, especially healthy fats and fresh fruit and vegetables.

EVERYONE'S DIFFERENT, AND I'M AS VALUABLE AS ANYONE ELSE.

IF I TRY SOMETHING AND IT DOESN'T WORK OUT, THAT'S OK.

I DON'T HAVE TO BE THE BEST AT EVERYTHING. I'M GOOD AT BEING ME!

SELF-ESTEEM

Self-esteem means how you feel about yourself. Having low self-esteem makes it hard to accept yourself. You might feel you can't do things, or that people won't like you. This can cause stress and anxiety, and can make life more difficult.

To develop good self-esteem, remember that no one is perfect, and it's OK to be who you are.

PERFORMANCE PSYCHOLOGY

Performance psychology means using psychology to help you do your best. It's used a lot in sports to help players get into the best state of mind for a competition. It's useful other places, too.

SPORTS PSYCHOLOGY

Playing a sport, especially at a high level, can be VERY stressful. You could be performing in front of a huge crowd, with TV cameras and the whole world watching. What you do at that moment could win or lose a game, a medal, or a world record.

A sports psychologist can help by training the player to cope with high-pressure moments. One method is to practice in noisy, stressful surroundings to help the player get used to it. The psychologist can also teach them how to stay calm and focused, using techniques like breathing exercises and CBT (see page 108).

PSYCHOLOGY AT WORK

Some jobs involve performing in front of other people, or stress from a heavy workload. Emergency and health workers often have to deal with upsetting or scary situations. Psychologists can help people learn to de-stress or to solve a problem that affects their work, such as a fear of public speaking.

Managers and bosses also use psychology to help them work with their staff. Different people have different personalities and working styles. Understanding and working with them helps them to do their best and feel happy at work.

Ed is a perfectionist. He works really hard, but he's always worrying that he's not good enough. He needs plenty of reassurance.

Emily has ADHD. She's a very good designer and gets totally absorbed in her work. She just needs a few reminders to stay on schedule.

AT SCHOOL

Educational psychologists work with schools to help students with their mental health. They can spot problems, arrange therapy, and work with teachers to help them understand.

INTO THE FUTURE

Sci-fi books and movies often feature amazing futuristic brain and mind science. Computers or robots think for themselves and take over the world. People scan each other's brains using mind-reading technology or control machines with their thoughts. Could things like this come true?

 ## MIND READING

Brain scientists have already developed basic mind-reading technology. It uses a combination of MRI scanning (see page 23) and neural networks (see page 97).

The MRI scanner scans someone's brain while they say different words.

The patterns of brain activity linked to each word or phrase are fed into a neural network in a computer, and it learns which patterns are linked to which words.

To test the system, the scanner picks up brain patterns while people think a sentence or story in their heads.

The computer program matches the brain patterns to its knowledge to decode what the person was thinking.

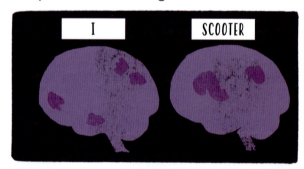

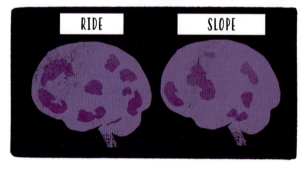

It's not very accurate yet and takes a long time. But eventually, we could use technology like this to control things like phones, computers, and household gadgets, using our thoughts.

OUT OF CURIOSITY
Is technology changing us?

Some psychologists and brain experts think the widespread use of the internet, smartphones, and social media is changing our brains and behavior.

On the plus side, we seem to be getting better at:

- Finding information quickly
- Using our brains for several things at once
- Interactive learning, using things like online quizzes and language lessons

But some experts think there are downsides, too:

- The average attention span—how long you can focus on one thing—is getting shorter.
- Many people feel they are more forgetful, since they can keep information on their phones or find it online whenever they need to, and use digital reminders to remember things.
- Social media can cause stress and anxiety, as people seek "likes" and compare themselves to others.

DISABILITY AIDS

Mind-reading technology could be especially useful for disabled people. For example, someone who is paralyzed and cannot move could use their mind to send words to a computer, which would turn them into speech.

There are already prosthetic (artificial) arms that connect to nerves in the body and link to the brain. The owner learns to control the arm using their thoughts, just like a real one.

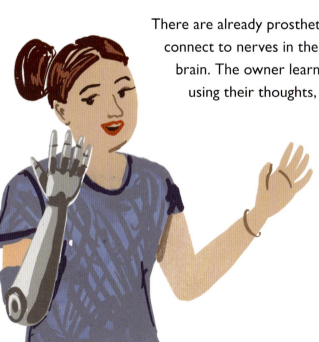

Scientists are also working on robotic body suits called exoskeletons, which allow people who are paralyzed to walk and do everyday activities using mind control.

Chapter 6

121

BRAIN EXPERIMENTS

Here's a selection of fun and fascinating illusions and experiments you can do at home. Try them out, and see if you can test, trick, or confuse your brain!

DOUBLE NOSE ILLUSION

This simple trick show how your brain makes sense of touch signals.

Cross your first and second fingers like this, so there's a gap between the tips.

Then, with both fingertips, rub the tip of your nose. It should feel as if you have two noses! But why?

Your brain knows the difference between the sides of your fingertips. If it gets touch signals from the outside edges of both fingers, it thinks there must be two separate objects. By crossing them over, you confuse your brain!

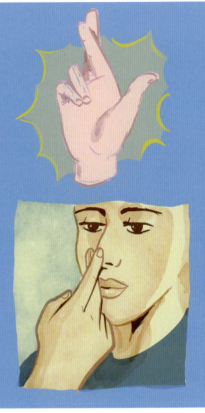

A HOLE IN YOUR HAND

This experiment shows how your brain combines the signals from both eyes.

You need a cardboard tube from a roll of paper towel, foil, or food wrap—or just roll up a piece of paper to make a tube.

Now put the end of the tube to one eye, and hold up your other hand next to it, about 10 cm (4 in) from your face. Keep both eyes open, and try to look through your hand.

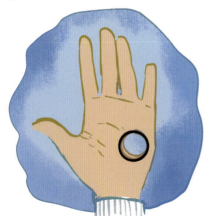

You should see a hole through your hand! One eye sees a hand, and the other sees the view out of the end of the tube. But the brain puts them together!

122

PONZO ILLUSION

This is a famous optical illusion that makes it hard for your brain to estimate sizes. Which car is the smallest? Which is the biggest? Measure them and see.

They're all the same size!
Thanks to years of experience, your brain knows that objects that look small are often farther away. The way the cars are parked and the shape of the road tells you they must be different distances away—but they're all the same size. Your brain interprets that to mean the farther away ones must be bigger!

TABLE ILLUSION

Here's another mind-blowing optical illusion. The tops of these two tables are the exact same size and shape. Don't believe it? To check, trace one tabletop, cut out the shape, and see if it fits over the other one.

Your brain knows that when it sees a table, the top looks narrower than it is really, because you usually see tables from the side, not from above. So it thinks that the long table is longer than it looks, and the wide table is wider than it looks.

HOT AND COLD

For this you need three mixing bowls or large food containers. Half fill one with hot tap water (not too hot to touch), one with cold water, and one with a medium-warm mixture of hot and cold. Put them on a table with the medium one in the middle.

Sit at the table, and put one hand in the cold water and the other in the hot water, and wait for 1 minute. Then take both hands out, and put them both in the middle bowl. How warm does the water feel?

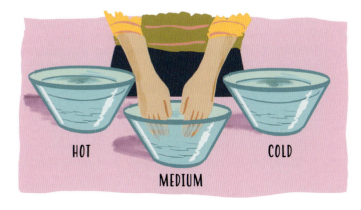

It should feel hot to one hand and cold to the other hand - even though it's the same water! We aren't actually very good at sensing temperatures. Instead, the brain and senses identify when we're warming up or cooling down. In this experiment, one hand is warming up, and the other is cooling down, so they experience the water differently.

Chapter 6

123

GLOSSARY

Alzheimer's disease: An illness that damages the brain, causing dementia.

Axon: The long part of a neuron, or nerve cell, that signals travel along.

Axon terminals: Branches on the end of an axon that pass signals to other neurons.

Bacteria: Very small, single-cell microorganisms, which can sometimes act as germs.

Bias: A tendency to prefer or select a particular idea, thing or person.

Big Five or Five-Factor model: A way of measuring personality based on five traits: extroversion, agreeableness, openness, conscientiousness and neuroticism.

Brain pruning: The way the brain reduces connections between neurons that are not needed.

Brain stem: The part of the brain that links it to the spinal cord.

Brain waves: Patterns of electrical activity in the brain.

Brain wiring: The way neurons are linked together to make the brain work.

Cells: The tiny units that living things are made up of.

Cerebellum: The lower back section of the brain, which helps to control balance and movement.

Cerebrum: The main part of the brain, which is covered with the cortex.

Clique: A small group or gang who exclude others from joining them.

Computer modeling or simulation: Using computer software to imitate real-life situations.

Conditioning: The way our behavior or thoughts are affected by learning from experiences.

Confirmation bias: Looking for evidence to support what you believe, while ignoring evidence that doesn't support it.

Conscious mind: The part of your mind that is aware of yourself and your thoughts.

Consciousness: Awareness of your own thoughts and existence, or being awake.

Cortex: The wrinkled outer layer covering most of the brain.

Data: Numbers and other results collected from doing experiments.

Deja vu: A sense of having experienced a situation in exactly the same way before.

Dementia: A loss of thinking ability, causing problems like forgetfulness and confusion.

Dendrites: Branch-shaped parts of neurons that receive signals from other neurons.

DNA (short for DeoxyriboNucleic Acid): A chemical found in cells, containing coded instructions that make the cell work.

Dualism: The idea that the body is separate from the mind, soul or spirit.

Electrons: Extremely tiny parts of atoms that move at high speed.

Epilepsy: An illness that affects electrical signalling in the brain.

Extrovert: Someone who feels energized and refreshed by being with others.

fMRI: (Short for functional Magnetic Resonance Imaging) A type of brain scan that shows which parts of the brain we use for different tasks.

Genes: Sequences of chemicals arranged along strands of DNA, which act as coded instructions for cells.

Glial cells: Cells in the brain that support the neurons and help them to work.

Gray matter: The pinkish-gray outer part of the brain, made up of the ends of lots of neurons linked together.

Groupthink: Making decisions or forming views as a group, instead of thinking for yourself.

Hemispheres: The two halves of the brain, left and right.

Hormones: Chemicals that can be released by the body to control how it works.

Hypothesis: A guess or idea about how something works, which can be tested with an experiment.

Impostor syndrome: A feeling of not being good enough or being a fake.

Inkblot tests: Personality tests based on the pictures that people see in random patterns of ink.

Instinct: A built-in, automatic pattern of behavior in an animal.

Introvert: Someone who feels energized and refreshed by spending time alone.

IQ (short for Intelligence Quotient): A measure of intelligence based on the ability to solve quiz questions and puzzles.

Lab: Short for laboratory, a room or building where scientists do tests or experiments.

Learning curve: The way learning slows down over time when we try to learn something new.

Limbic system: A group of organs in the middle of the brain that help to process memories, emotions and instinctive behavior.

Long-term memory: Memories that are saved from everyday life and stored for a long time in the brain .

Mental: To do with the mind.

Mental health: The health of the mind

Mental illness: An illness of the mind, affecting a person's emotions, behavior or beliefs.

Mind's eye: The ability most people have to create an image of something inside their head.

Muscle memory: Patterns of movements that we learn and remember, such as how to play an instrument or ride a bike.

Nature: A name for the way genes and DNA affect your body, mind and personality.

Nervous system: The brain and all the nerves that link it to the rest of the body.

Neural network: A type of computer software that imitates neuron connection and can learn from experience.

Neurodivergent: Having a brain that processes information differently from most people's.

Neurodiversity: The range of different types of brain wiring and information processing found in different people.

Neurons: Brain or nerve cells that carry signals around the brain and body and can form connections with each other.

Neuroscience: The study of the brain and nervous system

Neurotransmitters: Chemicals that help signals to travel around in the brain.

Nonverbal: Without speaking or words.

Norms: Ways of thinking or doing things that are expected or considered normal.

Nurture: A name for the way experiences and upbringing affect your body, mind and personality.

Pareidolia: The tendency to see faces or other pictures in random shapes or patterns.

Perception: Our awareness and understanding of what is going on around us.

Performance psychology: Using psychology to help people perform better, for example, in work, education, or sports.

Phantom limb: A sensation that an amputated limb or other body part is still there.

Philosophy: Studying or thinking about big questions such as the nature of reality, meaning, existence, or right and wrong.

Pineal gland: A brain part that releases hormones to control sleeping and waking.

Placebo effect: The way a placebo, or fake treatment or medicine, can improve people's health, even if they know it is fake.

Plasticity: The ability of the brain to change and form new neuron connections.

Prejudice: A view or judgement about a person without knowing them, based on things like their appearance, age, or disability.

Prosthetic: An artificial replacement body part, such as a robotic arm.

Puberty: A stage of growing up when you change from a child into an adult.

REM sleep: A stage of sleep when your eyes move rapidly, and most dreaming happens.

Scientific method: A way of planning and doing experiments to make sure they work and have accurate results.

Self-awareness: An awareness of your own personality, emotions, and behavior.

Self-esteem: A feeling of accepting yourself and believing you are worthwhile.

Self-image: The idea of yourself that you have in your mind.

Short-term memory: Information that you can keep in your conscious mind for a short time.

Spinal cord: A bundle of nerves that runs down the middle of the back, linking the brain stem to the rest of the body.

Stereotype: A way someone is expected to look or behave because of what group they belong to, such as their sex or where they are from.

Stigma: Disapproval or negativity from other people about a person or their behavior.

Stress: A feeling of mental pressure or being overloaded.

Stroke: A kind of brain damage that can happen when a blood vessel in the brain leaks or gets blocked.

Subconscious mind: The part of the mind where knowledge and memories are stored. They can be retrieved, but you don't constantly think about them.

Synapse: A tiny gap between two neurons at the point where signals pass between them.

Tribalism: A feeling of belonging and loyalty to a particular group and opposition to other groups.

Tumor: A lump that can grow in the brain or another body part.

Unconscious mind: The part of the mind that contains unconscious ideas and memories that you are not aware of.

Vocal cords: Stretchy bands of muscle in the throat that vibrate when you speak or sing.

White matter: The white inner part of the brain, made up of the axons or long central parts of neurons.

INDEX

adrenaline 102

ageing 76–9

Alzheimer's disease 79

amygdala 11

ancient times 46–7, 82–3

animal psychology 60–1, 86–7

anxiety 104, 106, 109, 111, 117, 121

Asch, Solomon 92

attention 91, 121

attention deficit hyperactivity disorder (ADHD) 22, 43, 119

autism 43

axons 12

Ayurveda 47

babies 68–9, 72, 88–9

behavior 45–61, 96

beta blockers 111

bias 59

bipolar disorder 104, 110

birds 61

body language 53

brain 5–25, 63, 109
  adult 74–5
  ageing 76–9
  animal 87
  baby's 68–9, 72
  caring for your 116–17
  blood flow 76, 79, 113
  development 68–9, 72
  evolution 64–5

experiments 81–99, 122–3

mysteries 25

myths 24

and the nature-nurture debate 66–7

and neurotransmitters 110

plasticity 71, 72

pruning 72

reward system 56

size 7, 78

and technology 120–1

teenage 72–3

wiring 42, 66

brain cells 5, 12–13

brain damage 112–113

brain scans 23, 120

brain stem 10

brain surgery 114–115

brain tumour 114

brain waves 23

breathing 28

Broca's area 11, 50

cerebellum 10, 19

cerebral hemispheres 10, 14, 24

cerebrum 10

change 63–79

child development 69–71, 72, 88–9, 107

chunking 95

Cognitive Behavioral Therapy (CBT) 109

computer models 96–97

computers 33

conditioning 86

confirmation bias 59

conformity 92–93

conscious mind 28, 29

consciousness 25, 33

copying 70

cortex 10–12, 17, 19, 23, 73–4

daydreams 32–33

deja vu 25

dementia 79, 83

dendrites 12, 15

depression 104, 109

Descartes, René 48

diet, healthy 111, 117

digit span tests 95

disability aids 121

DNA 42, 66–67, 106

dogs 60–61

dopamine 110

dreaming 20–21

drugs, recreational 117

dualism 25

Dunbar's number 49

dyslexia 43

dyspraxia 43

ears 16, 17

eating disorders 105

Ebbinghaus, Hermann 94

educational psychology 119

emotional intelligence (EQ) 41

emotions 6, 36–38, 52, 60, 69, 73

encoding 25

endorphins 109, 110

environment 31, 107

epilepsy 22, 83, 114

evolutionary psychology 64–65

eyes 17, 20, 76

facial expressions 52–53, 60

fear 35, 37, 61, 64

feature integration 91

Fechner Color Effect 83

feedback 49

"fight or flight" response 35

filtering 17, 91

fitting in (belonging) 56

foetal development 68, 88

four humours 46–47

Freud, Sigmund 29

frontal lobe 74, 113

functional Magnetic Resonance
Imaging (fMRI) 23

future, the 120–121

Gage, Phineas 112–113

genes 42, 66–7, 106

glial cells 12

gray matter 13

groups 54–57, 92–93

group identity 48

groupthink 57

growth 63–79

hearing 11, 16, 17, 24, 90

"hidden gorilla" study 91

hippocampus 11, 19, 76

Homo sapiens 65

hypothalamus 11, 20

hypotheses 84

ideas, sharing 51

illusory correlations 58

imposter syndrome 74

individual differences 42

instinct 61, 69

intelligence 40–41, 87

Intelligence Quotient (IQ) 40–41

language 6, 11, 23, 33, 36, 50–51,
70–71, 88

leadership 77, 119

learning 76, 79

learning curves 94

life experience 75, 107, 108

lifestyle 107, 116–117

limbic system 11, 69, 73

logic 71

McGurk Effect 90

Magnetic Resonance Imaging (MRI)
23, 120

medicines 110–111

memory 18–19, 30–31

content 18

linked 30

long-term 18

memory-matching 34–35

mistakes 31, 34

problems 76, 121

short-term 18

tests 94–95

working 18

meninges 112, 115

mental health/illnesses 101–123

causes 106–107

medicines 110–111

therapies 108–109

types of disorder 104–105

microscopes 22

mind 5–7, 25, 27–43, 48, 63, 77

mind-reading technology 120–121

mirrors 98

mistakes, making 58–59

motor function 11, 15

muscle relaxants 111

muscles 52

music 24, 42

nature-nurture debate 66–67

nervous system 14–15, 66, 83

peripheral 14

nervousness 36

neural networks 97, 120

neurodiversity 22, 42–43

neurons 12–13, 15, 19–20, 22–23,
25, 42–43, 78, 97

neuroplasticity 71, 72

neuroscience 7, 22–23

neurotransmitters 110

Index

127

nonverbal communication 52–53

norms 56

Obsessive-Compulsive Disorder (OCD) 105–106, 109

optical illusions 35, 122–123

pain 15

panic 104, 111

paralysis 121

pareidolia 35

patterns 58

Pavlov's dogs 86

perception 34–35, 90–91

performance psychology 118–119

personality 38–39, 46–47, 93, 112–113

phantom limbs 25

phobias 105, 109

physical activity 79, 109, 116–117

placebo effect 99

plaques 79

Ponzo illusion 123

Post-Traumatic Stress Disorder (PTSD) 105, 109

prefrontal cortex 11, 19, 23, 73

prejudice 57

prosthetic limbs 121

puberty 72–73, 74

reaction times 83

reflexes 15

relationships 48–49

responsibility 74–75

rewards 56

risk-taking 74

robotic suits 121

roles 55, 75

Rorschach inkblot tests 39

Sally Anne test 89

schizophrenia 105, 106, 110

Schwann cells 12

scientific method 81

scientists, influence of 93

self, sense of 48–49

self-awareness 49

self-esteem 117

self-image 48–49, 73

sensory system 11, 15–17, 23–24, 30, 34–35, 66, 71, 83, 90–91, 99, 113, 122–123

serotonin 110

sleep 20–21, 117

non-REM 21

REM 20–21

sleeping pills 111

smell, sense of 11, 30

social language 51

social media 121

social psychology 54–57, 92–93, 116

speech 50–51

spinal cord 14–15

sports psychology 118

stereotypes 57

stigma 56

stress 75, 102–103, 107, 109, 111, 116–119, 121

strokes 113, 114

Stroop test 98

subconscious mind 28, 29

suprachiasmatic nucleus (SCN) 20–21

synaesthesia 43

synapses 13, 78

synaptic pruning 72

talking therapies 108

teenagers 72–73

temperature, sensing 123

thalamus 11

theory of mind 89

thinking 6–7, 32–33, 73

three doshas 47

time perception 35

"tip-of-tongue" syndrome 30

trepanning 110

tribalism 55

unconscious mind 28, 29

ventricles 787

vision 11, 17, 23, 83, 90–91, 99, 113, 122–123

Wernicke's area 11, 50

white matter 13

workplaces 119

Wundt, William 83